The Library of Literature

Under the General Editorship of
JOHN HENRY RALEIGH & IAN WATT

One Hundred
Middle English Lyrics

THE LIBRARY OF LITERATURE

One Hundred
Middle English Lyrics

EDITED

WITH AN INTRODUCTION BY
ROBERT D. STEVICK

University of Washington

THE **BOBBS-MERRILL** COMPANY, INC.
A SUBSIDIARY OF HOWARD W. SAMS & CO., INC.
Publishers • INDIANAPOLIS • NEW YORK

INTRODUCTION

The origins of Middle English lyric verse are obscure. Because the technique and form of the earliest known poems in Middle English differ significantly from those of Old English verse, no direct line from the earlier verse to the later can be traced. Moreover, the early Middle English lyrics do not appear to represent a rudimentary stage of lyric development. We are therefore compelled to accept one of three inferences of their origin: a spontaneous generation and development so rapid as to leave no trace of its beginnings; a borrowing or imitation of verse compositions in another language and from another culture; or a gradual process of development, perhaps subject to influence through borrowing from another source, that is not apparent in writings of the time which are extant.

The nature and known history of art forms offer no support to the first inference. The second, however, is conceivable. Borrowing and imitation may occur when two cultures are closely associated; they are perhaps more likely to occur in nonlanguage arts or in fully literary—that is, lettered—art forms. But much of the earliest lyric verse in English seems to have belonged mainly to the unlettered segment of society, and evidence to establish a clear foreign cultural source for it is insufficient. The third inference, that of a longer native development possibly influenced from without, is the most plausible.

We do know, for example, that many of the earliest lyric poems, known from surviving fragments and references, were the words of popular songs and sayings of uneducated, unlettered people. The earliest fragments are quoted in such sources as sermons condemning the behavior that accompanied the songs—dancing, especially in churchyards; games and other enjoyments of pleasures of the flesh; non-Christian celebrations; and so on. When texts are numerous and complete enough to give some basis for comparison, it seems clear that many poems were perpetuated orally rather than in writing. There was, of course, no publication of texts. However, some texts apparently were composed in writing and propagated through copies or memorization of written versions. From the beginning these were mostly religious, often didactic, compositions. Subsequently, among the preserved texts, the popular oral verse seems to disappear, and poems of poets, properly so called, remain as the principal texts of which we have record. This development suggests that the lyric verse of England has origins that are lowly, popular, and undisciplined (or noninstitutionalized) but tells us little that is more specific or substantial than that. The one exception is the carol, which in many instances has individual authorship and is "popular by destination" rather than by origin.

At the latter end of its history, the Middle English lyric form and its influence on later English poetry are difficult to trace. The rise to fashion of self-consciously educated poets, adopting modes, forms, themes, and techniques from foreign literatures, and experimenting a great deal, caused the earlier kind of verse to decline. So did the rise of conditions favoring individual authorship, reading, and, hence, fixed texts; printing is a major example. Some continuity can be traced, of course. Themes of spring, love, and death persist. Conventions of address, the catalog, and the farewell are not lost. Accentual meter, use of rhyme, and a penchant for alliteration continued. Allusion to the Bible is constant. There is an occasional closer resemblance between verses of the successive eras, like that between No. **62** in this collection and I.ix.40 of *The Faerie Queene*. But continuity in English culture and in the structure of the English language does not constitute influence. A literate, self-conscious tradition of educated poets superseded the homely, religious, and unself-conscious tradition of the makers of Middle English lyric verse. In literature, the Renaissance displaced the Middle Ages.

The literary texts collectively labeled "Middle English lyrics" are so varied in nature that a general description of them must be limited to a few rather broad characteristics. About the only features common to all these texts are that they employ rhyme and (nearly always) iambic meter and that they are relatively short, not predominantly narrative, single in subject, and "medieval" in tone.

If general description is somewhat vague, classification of the texts is hardly more definitive. Several classifications have been made, to be sure; but completeness and consistency of any single classification results from ignoring more aspects of the poems than are used to group them. Division of the texts into "secular" and "religious" is the most common way of classifying them. Since all subjects of the poems can with some justification be listed under one or the other of these heads, this classification is systematically respectable. However, the compartmentalizations to which style, verse form, theme, and other facets of the poems yield are not at all congruent with classification by the nature of the subject matter. And if any means of classifying can reflect the historical development of Middle English lyric verse, it is not that of subject but those of style, form, theme, tone, and recurrent phrases or formulas.

I.

Two factors account for the inaccessibility of Middle English lyrics to all but a small class of medievalists and specialists in English philology. First, the English language in the thirteenth, fourteenth, fifteenth centuries consisted of a variety of dialects, differing widely and changing rapidly, and it lacked an established standard dialect for literary composition. More than one writer at the time deplored the situation. Poems were written down in the speech of the writer, reflecting his own pronunciation and inflectional patterns, and spelling was based on the particular system of orthography he had inherited or developed. As a result, almost every manuscript preserving lyric poems from this period differs to some extent in dialect or spelling from all others.

Second, no comprehensive collection of Middle English lyric verse is linguistically uniform. Lyric verse for the most part was indifferently preserved when the poems were current. Subsequent preservation was left less to custom than to caprice for four hundred years or more—until historical interests in the texts became institutionalized, as much for philological as for literary reasons. The larger and better manuscript collections are local in dialect and limited in scope; no cumulative collection of lyric poems from the latter part of the Middle English period is extant. We have, then, several hundred lyric poems in texts that are diverse in dialect and irregular in notation, which remain beyond the reach of most modern readers.

Because many of the lyrics possess considerable intrinsic merit in addition to their historical value for the study of English poetry, they should be made generally accessible. Short of asking every potential reader of Middle English lyrics to serve an apprenticeship to the trade of philology, there appear to be only two modes of accomplishing this goal: to translate the texts into Modern English or to regularize them to some extent in Middle English itself.

The first alternative has frequently proved unsatisfactory. Translation, especially of lyric verse, is a difficult art at best. It becomes almost impossible when the cultural circumstances from which a poem derives differ more from our own than the language—or the appearance of the language—of the original poem differs from Modern English. Often, for instance, a word has survived with no change in form (especially written form) that is comparable to the change in its meaning or associations—yet one cannot substitute a modern term without doing violence to the delicate and precise complex that is a "good" lyric poem. Then, too, the meter of Middle English lyrics depends to some extent on the syllabic nature of inflectional endings that no longer exist, even though spelling may not always reflect their disappearance. Modernization of spelling and substitution of cognates is often used in translation. This, however, produces a text in neither Modern nor Middle

English and seldom conveys anything like the qualities of the original poem. Certainly, no appreciable number of these lyrics has been rendered successfully in Modern English; and the number of translations that are similar in technique and equal in skill is insufficient for a collection.

The other alternative for resolving the language barrier of Middle English dialects is to effect some measure of regularization. The Chambers and Sidgwick *Early English Lyrics* (see List of Abbreviations, page xxix), adopts this course for printing poems from the early thirteenth century up to the advent of the sonnet. "The ground covered is so wide as to render three different modes of treating the orthography desirable. Poems written before 1400 are left practically in the spelling of the scribes; those of the fifteenth century are slightly normalised...; those still later are altogether modernised" (page ix). R. T. Davies' *Medieval English Lyrics* (1963), which appeared after these pages were set in type, adopts an eclectic method of modifying spelling (see pages 48-49).

The present volume follows the second alternative, but its method differs from that of Chambers and Sidgwick. Texts of lyric verse of the thirteenth, fourteenth, and fifteenth centuries are presented here in a single Middle English written dialect: they have been normalized as fully as possible to the emerging literary dialect of Chaucer and his contemporaries of the London–East Midland region at about 1400 (the procedure used in normalizing the texts is described on pages xvi–xx). This specific dialect has been selected for historical as well as practical reasons. Historically, it stands near the line of development of Modern Standard English and probably is the dialect of more of the Middle English verse now commonly read than any other. Practically, it is sufficiently near the "center" of Middle English dialects—systematically considered—to render verse selected from scattered regions and divergent centuries with a minimum of modification. Inflectional suffixes, for example, whether metrically syllabic or assimilated or elided, nearly always find precedent in Chaucer's poetry. Though nouns usually have -*es* plural inflection in the stipulated dialect, -*en* alternates with -*es* in some instances and would readily be comprehended in others, when required to maintain rhyme. No less of practical value is the acquaintance of most potential readers of these poems with some of Chaucer's works, at the least. The fluency in London–East Midland dialect of 1400 that a reader may bring to these lyric poems should give him access to a generous collection of Middle English lyrics. Lacking moderate acquaintance with Chaucer's English, the reader still is able by the uniformity of these texts to develop efficiently a facility in reading them.

Taken in all, the texts presented here, separately and as a collection, are offered as facts of literary history, although they are not literally factual in the strict historical sense of being exact transcripts of extant documents of the period they represent. In this respect they are similar to texts in Modern English editions of Milton, Malory, or Shakespeare. They are necessary and useful, however, in ways not shared by editions bringing Early Modern English texts into twentieth-century English, and may even have superior justification in filling a hiatus that is historically conceivable. If there had been a compiler, like the one who left us MS. Digby 86 or MS. Harley 2253, but who was born about 1380 in the East Midlands; if he had lived in or near London for several years and, while traveling about England near middle age, had indulged his fondness for lyric verse, seeking out, copying, and memorizing poems; if, then, upon returning home, he had written out a fair copy and perhaps handed it on to "his owne scriveyn, for to wryten newe": this quite credible citizen would then have left us his collection that, we may suppose, would not be unlike two-thirds of the one which follows. A continuator two generations later, imitating the collection already begun, could have supplied the rest.

It will be apparent, then, that this collection is intended to complement rather than to displace the scholarly editions of texts transcribed and edited directly from the manuscripts. Because its orientation is literary and because it is intended for the general reader and undergraduate rather than for the medievalist or specialist in English philology, this book differs from most collections not only in the language of the texts but also in format and in some aspects of selection and arrangement of texts.

II.

In selecting poems for this volume, I have sought to represent the tradition of Middle English lyric verse by illustrating its development and principal characteristics from the earliest period from which texts are preserved to the end of the fifteenth century. Most of the poems are anonymous; several are fragmentary; all are pre-Renaissance in character as well as date. As many of the best poems are included as the aim of representativeness allows. At the same time examples of the range of forms, conventions, themes, subjects, methods of adaptation, and qualities of execution are provided, the choice suggests something of the nature of some principal collections made during the Middle English period itself. For example, the best collection, in MS. Harley 2253, is represented here by Nos. 18 and 26 through 35. Some additional tags and bits, labeled here "Selected Fragments" (pages 174–175), typify poems—mostly songs—that have been lost but through these fragments are known to have existed. If all aspects cannot be fully or equally represented, at least their diversity and the recurrence of some are illustrated, and the collection as a whole parallels the scope of standard essays dealing with the Middle English lyric.

The texts are arranged in broadly chronological order. As hinted earlier, such other arrangements as grouping according to one or another classification have the disadvantage of drawing attention to only one aspect of the poems—the theme, the tone, the religious or secular nature of subject, or the like. They distract attention from other characteristics that may be of greater interest. Chronological arrangement at least avoids this fault, though it raises difficulties in itself. The date of a manuscript may be much later than that of composition or first general currency of a poem; occurrence of a poem in multiple texts of different half-centuries, as well as linguistic tests, exhibits this circumstance in several cases. Thus, the dates given for poems, and their place in the sequence, are only approximations. Some dates could be accurate to within two or three years; others may be accurate only to within fifty years. Even so, chronological arrangement makes apparent the main factors of lyrical development for the period.

Two common ingredients of editions of lyric verse of the Middle English period—descriptive and classificatory comments and appreciative remarks on the poems—have been omitted from this collection. It will be as apparent to any reader as to an editor that, for example, some of the poems are secular and others religious. Labeling or grouping, as has been pointed out, predisposes a reader to any given poem without sharpening his sense of discovery that many verse forms, structural conventions, and even lines and phrases are shared by secular and religious verse. Text **61** in this collection is secular in style but religious in statement. The conventional opening "As I walked through a greenwood one day recently" has a variety of uses, as does the formal device of addressing one's lady or lover; the formulaic structure "I asked X what she meant" recurs; identical lines occur in several poems. Of particular interest is the request for "thyn ore"—addressed to a sweetheart, a noble lady, the Virgin Mary, God, Christ, and the infant Jesus. These and many more aspects of the poems are sometimes better recorded, sorted out, and evaluated in the readers' notes than in the editor's.

Appreciative remarks, explications, critical analyses, and assessments of the poems have also been withheld. Their combination with poems in one physical volume would tend to fix the editor's interpretations on the poems, overshadowing other interpretations, including the reader's. It is perhaps enough that the editor has his say in the selection, arrangement, punctuation, and glossing of texts. This does not imply, of course, a sanction of the romantic attitude that one interpretation is as good as another or that untutored judgments possess a special virtue. It merely implies that a reader's active intelligence is to be respected as much as his receptive capacities.

Editorial help other than normalization of language and selection and arrangement of texts is provided for readers meeting lyric verse in Middle English for the first time. The text source is given for each poem as a footnote, as is the number under which the poem is listed in Carleton Brown and Rossell Hope Robbins, *The Index of Middle English Verse*. Because the poems have been chosen from "standard" editions usually available in college and larger public libraries, extensive notes and references have not been included; many of the standard editions are listed in the Abbreviations of Titles (page xxix). Bibliographic help is generally available in John E. Wells, *A Manual of the Writings in Middle English, 1050-1400* (1916), with supplements, and in the annual bibliography published in *PMLA* (Publications of the Modern Language Association of America). Glossing of the texts is calculated to suit both the initiated and the less skilled reader. "Hard words" occurring infrequently or words used with specialized meanings are glossed on the page where they occur; words that are less difficult or more common appear in the Glossary at the end of the volume. The printing of carols follows usual editorial practice of giving the burden only once, at the head of the poem. An exception is made in the case of the first carol in this collection (No. 25), when the burden is printed after each of the verses, representing the carol as it would be sung. The integral nature of the burden and verse recommends this, together with appropriate punctuation, for the sense of the poem. No. 85 reprints the burden at the end, for reasons that can readily be inferred. The language of the texts and the metrical features of the verses are described in the remaining portion of this Introduction.

III.

In describing the linguistic traits of this edition of Middle English lyrics, I thought it advisable to attempt to reach two levels of readers at once: the less experienced readers of Middle English; and those who, as mentors of the first group, may prefer a more technical and detailed discussion of the language and the problems of normalization.

The rapid, varied, and random mutations of spelling in Middle English can hardly be said to constitute a system at all, and the original texts of the lyric verses embody a generous sampling of the regional, chronological, and arbitrary differences in spelling practices. When *wh-* was generally replacing *hw-*, for example, *quh-* and *hu-* were regional variants (Scottish and Kentish), and *w-* was a (French) scribal variant for representing /hw/.[1] For poems in this collection, the opening pair of lines for No. 13 read, in manuscript: "Wose seye on rode / ihesus is lef-mon"; for No. 14A: "Wenne hic soe on rode idon / ihesus mi leman"; for No. 14B: "Quanne hic se on rode / ihesu mi lemman"; for No. 15: "Vyen i o þe rode se /Faste nailed to þe tre"; for No. 16: "Qvanne I zenke onne þe rode / quorupe-one þu stode." Spelling variations of these kinds contribute to linguistic decisions of date and provenance of the manuscript texts, as well as to pronunciation of the various dialects; but skill in interpreting such spellings obviously requires special training beyond the scope of time and interest of general readers of English literature.

Accordingly, in this edition, the irregularities among spelling

---

[1] Italics indicate spelling. Slant lines to enclose symbols indicate phonemic notation. A phoneme is a class of speech sounds contrasting with other speech sounds in a language, by which one thing that may be said is distinguished from anything else that might have been said. Thus, the meanings of Middle English /herə/ "hear," /werə/ "were," and /hendə/ "gracious," /wendə/ "go, turn" are distinguished by *h*-sounds and *w*-sounds—the phonemes /h/ and /w/.

conventions have been removed. Most of them, of course, are eliminated by adoption of a single written dialect. However consistent the spelling of a specific text may be, though, a dialect did not have anything approaching an ideal spelling system even when a dominant scribal tradition was established with it. The sources of spelling devices were English and French scribal conventions, whose separate inconsistencies and inadequacies multiplied when the traditions mingled, then stabilized, then were revised in endless and complex sequences. The copying of manuscripts of one dialect by a scribe who spoke (and wrote, by habit) another dialect was not always a mechanical procedure and contributed further variations within texts.

The result was that spelling, even for one dialect, was not clearly phonetic or phonemic or altogether fixed. Stressed vowels of like quality and quantity, for example, were represented by more than one letter or combination of letters, and the same letter or letter combination often represented more than one vowel—a situation not uncommon in Modern English either. The Chaucerian vowel closest in pronunciation to the vowel of Modern English *day* was spelled *e* as in *swete* "sweet," or *ee* as in *feet* "feet." These two spellings also represented the Chaucerian vowel closest to the vowel of Modern English *help*: *deel* "deal" and *eten* "eat."

To some extent, however, the spelling was fixed. Most morphemes[2] in a single scribal tradition were usually spelled in the same way, and those that were not usually had only two alternate spellings. Some (not all) morphophonemic variations (for example, *wyf*, *wyves*) had established spellings.

In light of these factors, the mode of spelling for the texts

---

[2] A morpheme, broadly defined, is a class of forms having a meaning distinguishable from meanings of other forms within a language. It is made up of one or more segmental phonemes (vowels and consonants), and contains only one meaningful unit. In Middle English, /bileyv-/*bileve* is one morpheme; /bileyvəθ/*bileveth* consists of two —a stem morpheme and a suffix morpheme /əθ/ used as an inflection. /bi/*by* is a separate morpheme, as is /leyv-/ *leve*, because their meanings are different from the meaning of /bileyv-/. Derivational forms are also morphemic, as /-nessə/ *-nesse* and /un-/*un-*.

of the lyrics in this collection was decided as follows: Since a phonetic or phonemic system of spelling, with one-to-one correspondence of written symbol and speech element, would have created texts more formidable in appearance than their extant manuscript versions, a single model was adopted—the Chaucerian texts. These texts provide a highly desirable model. They supply a large body of data, were influential in their own time, have established manuscript preferences, and are perhaps the most familiar today of the extensive Middle English texts in a single dialect. Equally important is their wealth and scope of vocabulary: a remarkable coextensiveness exists between their lexicon and that of the lyric verse of the time. Except for words predominantly Northern in provenance (usually Scandinavian in origin), Chaucer's texts contain most of the words occurring in these lyrics, often in identical idioms.

Using Chaucerian texts as a model entails certain operations and decisions. Determination of the Chaucerian spelling(s) of each morpheme is one; these were established by reference to *A Concordance to the Complete Works of Geoffrey Chaucer*. When alternate spellings appear (as they often do), the more frequent spelling is ordinarily adopted. When alternate spellings are distributed less with contrasting frequencies but generally according to texts—*e*, for example, in *Troilus and Criseyde* corresponding to *ee* in *The Canterbury Tales*—the spelling was fixed according to the historical trend of the phonemic make-up of the word and its spelling, or the convenience of eliminating homographs. See, for example, *seen, sene* in the Glossary (page 181). In sum, the spelling for the texts of the lyrics is modeled on Chaucer's texts, morpheme by morpheme, with spelling usually fixed on a single alternant when alternate spellings are common.

The most extensive effects of fixing on one alternate spelling are seen in the representation of "long" vowels. Reduplication of vowel letters is eliminated except with *ee* and *oo*. The spelling of /oh/, /ow/ and /eh/, /ey/—the so-called open and close "ō" and "ē"—was a special problem not solved very easily or simply. The trend of reduplication, finally limited to *ee* and *oo*, was established particularly at London and Oxford to indicate "long" vowels of the "e" and "o" series. The procedure was not regular, however, as the manuscripts of Chaucer's work show. For instance, the *Concordance* conveniently shows that more words than not have reduplicated vowel letters in *The Canterbury Tales* citations, when corresponding citations from *Troilus and Criseyde* spell with a single vowel letter. In general, the problem has been resolved for the texts of these lyrics in the following manner: close $\underline{\bar{o}}$ is spelled *oo* only when in a closed syllable; open $\underline{o}$ is spelled without reduplication; and both close and open $\underline{\bar{e}}$ are spelled *ee* only when in final position or when in a closed syllable. Otherwise *e* is given.

As described so far, this spelling policy is quite neat and regular. Just when a syllable should be considered open or closed, however, must sometimes be decided on the basis of meter or etymon. For example, a syllable may be open or closed according to whether a following (written) -*e*, representing (at least historically) an inflectional suffix, should be regarded as syllabic or not. In some dialects, double forms—with and without pronounced -*e*—were in use, as they were in literary texts of London in 1400. When the problem arises, Chaucer's texts have been consulted and the metrical structure of the line has been considered. In addition, there inevitably have been a few exceptions in spelling long *e* and *o*, principally for words of great frequency. By the rule given above, *dōn*, for example, would be spelled *doon* and *bē(n)* spelled *bee(n)*; yet they are spelled *don* and *be(n)*, and their derivative forms are spelled accordingly—*doth*, *beth*, etc.—to conform to usual scribal practice. On the other hand, *ōn* (OE *ān*) is regularly spelled *oon; too* "toe" (OE *tā*) occurs once.

Regularization includes fixing on such spellings as *awey*, *than* "then," *hir* "her," *her* "their." Other editorial customs are maintained: *u / v* and *i / j* are distinguished as vowel and consonant; any letters not in the Modern English alphabet have been transliterated. In addition, vocalic *i* and *y* do not alternate in any given root morpheme; *i*- is used as the past participial prefix, *y*- as the general (vestigial) verbal prefix.

Throughout this edition modern conventions of punctuation have been used. Standard editions of each text have been consulted and, usually, followed, but I have departed from their punctuation when syntactic and rhetorical structures can be more precisely indicated or when I have interpreted them differently.

In this edition, the paradigmatic classes are uniformly represented, for the same purposes as regularization of spelling and by similar means, so far as precedent of the model texts or general lines of linguistic history permit. The morphological descriptions that follow therefore resemble those drawn up for Chaucer's works, for example, W. W. Skeat's Oxford *Chaucer*, Vol. VI.

A. *Personal Pronouns*

I	my, myn	me
thou, -ow	thy, thyn	thee
he	his,	him
she	hir, hires	hire
it	his	it
we	oure, oures	us
ye	youre, youres	you
they	her, heres	hem

All pairs are used here in complementary distribution. *My / myn* and *thy / thyn* are distributed according to the initial sound of the following word if it is part of the same grammatical unit: *my faire swete herte, thy neighebore, myn owene lyf, thyn ore,* but also *myn herte, thyn hond.* When not preceding the noun they modify, *myn, thyn, oures, youres, heres, hires* are usual forms. Also, *myn, thyn* have inflectional *-e* for plural; occasionally in the earlier texts *hir* and *her* retain etymological (or analogical) *-e* of the source-text, as in No. **53,** line 8.

B. *Nouns*

$\{\emptyset\}$[3]	oon	sone	oon	flour	his	deeth
$\{S_1\}$	three	sones	three	floures	her	dethes
$\{S_2\}$	his	sones sorwe	the	floures savour		dethes wither-clench

The first member of this paradigm, $\{\emptyset\}$ (i.e., no suffix) is the singular morpheme, contrasting with $\{S_1\}$, the plural morpheme; $\{S_2\}$ is variously called "genitive," "determinative," "possessive." As many infrequent inflectional allomorphs (*i.e.*, alternate forms of a morpheme) are eliminated in the texts as evidence and structure of the poetic line permit. Occasionally, however, a fourth member of the paradigm occurs, often in frequent or formulaic phrases corresponding to Old English dative inflections; it has the shape /-ə/ *-e*, as in *wyth childe* (**10.**12), *in boure* (**29.**1), *to grounde* (**35.**6). Also, the plural morpheme $\{S_1\}$, which nearly always had the shape /-əs/, included allomorphs /-ən/ *-en* and /$\emptyset$/. These occurred with some frequency, as in Chaucer's *eyen* "eyes," for example. Consequently, *-en* plurals are retained when rhymes require them. While Chaucer consistently wrote *woundes*, for instance, he would have understood *wounden* immediately. *Thyng* is a frequent instance of plural with /$\emptyset$/ inflection and cannot always be replaced by *thynges* (cf. **19.**8, **27.**6). A notable problem in dealing with noun-plural allomorphs arises in these texts with the root *hond* "hand." Middle English forms are *honde*, *hondes, honden, hend(e)*. While *hend(e)* is not used in this edition, rhyme and meter dictate alternation of other forms. For example, with *honde*, but not with *hondes*, the inflectional suffix can be elided with certain following words, reducing the plural of *hond* to a monosyllable, for metrical purposes.

[3] Braces { } indicate a symbol representing a morpheme and all its allomorphs. $\emptyset$, read "zero," indicates absence of an overt form.

A few double forms of roots occur, such as *wyl, wylle;* usually these forms continue double forms that had occurred in Old English.

C. *Adjectives*

Generally, monosyllabic adjectives, *myn, thyn,* and a few others, show the following inflectional characteristics:

a good man

the / that / thy gode man

Come, gode man, . . .

gode men

thyn hond	al my lyf	swich a dede
thyne hondes	alle her lyves	swiche dedes

D. *Verbs*

The personal inflections of verbs need not be listed here in full, since they are regular and offer no difficulty, but the plural *-en* (alternating with *-e*) may be mentioned. Tense inflections, similarly, correspond closely to those of Modern English; exceptions are those of some "strong" verbs, and these are listed and cross-referenced in the Glossary. In nearly every instance, verbs with both strong and weak forms have been made either strong or weak. The forms of anomalous and irregular verbs are also given in the Glossary. Modal inflections are as follows. Imperative singular Ø (no suffix), or *-e* for some weak verbs, plural *-(e)th,* rarely *-e.* Present subjunctive singular *-e,* plural *-e(n);* preterite subjunctive is similar, except that there may be no inflectional suffix after *-(e)d.* Infinitive inflections are *-e* or *-en.* Participial forms are sufficiently similar to those of Modern English to cause no difficulty.

E. *Adverbs, prepositions, particles, demonstrative and inter-rogative pronouns.*

These, if not closely similar to those of Modern English, are listed in the Glossary.

Whether or not the phonetic reconstructions of Middle English dialects correspond exactly to the speech of the time, it is necessary to have some pronunciation system in order to read Middle English texts fluently. A pronunciation system that is deliberately designed to reflect the phonemic structure of the stipulated dialect is preferable to most improvisations of users of Modern English only. On these grounds, the following guide is offered.

The consonants are these:

/p/	pere, hap	*as Mod. E.*	*peer*
/t/	tere, but		*tear*
/č/	chere, wrecched		*cheer*
/k/	kyn, care, quene, pak, six		*kin*
/f/	fere, staf		*staff*
/θ/	there, lieth		*thin*
/s/	so, certeyn, aske, lesse, six		*so*
/š/	sholde, fresshe		*should*
/b/	bere, neb		*bear*
/d/	dere, bed		*dear*
/j/	daunger, juggement		*judge*
/g/	gon, agulte		*go*
/v/	vale, staves		*vale*
/ð/	blithe		*blithe*
/z/	rose, lese		*rose*
/x/	soghte, thoght, thogh		——
/h/	here, herte		*hear*
/w/	were, sorwe		*were*

/m/	mere, am	as Mod. E.	*mill*
/l/	lere, al		*like*
/j/	yeer, ayeins		*year*
/n/	nere, an, signe		*near*
/r/	rede, bour		*rear*

It should be noticed that /ŋ/ and /ž/ as in Modern English *sing* and *azure* were not phonemic in Middle English, and that /x/ is not part of the Modern English phonemic system.[4] Double consonant letters indicate lengthened consonants; in some instances, such as *sone* "son," *sonne* "sun," length is phonemic.

The chart opposite, which draws heavily on Chapter IV of Samuel Moore's *Historical Outlines of English Sounds and Inflections* (revised by Albert H. Marckwardt, 1951) and Chapter 43 of Charles F. Hockett's *A Course in Modern Linguistics* (1958), offers a correlation between the stressed vowels of these lyric texts and those of Modern English that may be helpful.

Word stress, when different from that of corresponding Modern English forms, can be inferred from the metrical stress patterns.

Normalization of all the following texts to the incipient literary dialect of London–East Midlands at about 1400 requires a brief statement of the relation of normalization and emendation in this edition. Normalization of texts may be broadly stipulated to consist of (1) reshaping morphemes of a text in one dialect to conform to the shape of their correlatives in another and, in some inflections, using the expected allomorphs of one dialect in place of those occurring in texts from another dialect; and (2) adoption of a stable spelling practice (uniform morphographs). "When þe nyhtegale singes" is normalized to "Whan the nyghtengale syngeth" (32.1). Normalization is

---

[4] /x/ is distinguished phonetically as a voiceless velar or palatal spirant. Roughly, as [t] is to [θ], so [k] is to [x].

Phoneme	Spelling	Pronunciation		If Modern English has	
			as in		as in
/i/	i, y	[ɪ]	drynke, bidde	[ɪ]	drink, bid
/e/	e	[ɛ]	helpe	[ɛ]	help
/a/	a	[a]	can	[æ]	can
/o/	o	[ɔ]	oxe	[a]	ox
/u/	u, o	[ʊ]*	under, sone	[ʌ]	under, son
/iy/	i, y	[iː]	side, wyf	[aɪ]	side, wife
/ey/	e, ee	[eː]*	sweet, feet	[iː]	sweet, feet
/ay/	ai, ay, ei, ey	[æɪ]*	day, pleye	[e] or [eɪ]	day, play
/oy/	oi, oy	[ɔɪ]	boy, vois	[ɔɪ]	boy, voice
/iw/	u, eu, ew	[ɪʊ] or [ɛʊ]	pure, dewe	[ɪu, u] or [ju]	pure, dew
/aw/	o, ou, ow, au, aw	[ɔʊ] or [aʊ]	thoght, taughte, sawe	[ɔ]	thought, taught, saw
/ow/	o, oo	[oː]*	fode, mood	[u]	food, mood
/uw/	ou, ow	[uː]*	hous	[aʊ]	house
/eh/	e, ee	[æː]*	lede, seed	[iː]	lead, seed
/ah/	a, aa	[aː]*	name, aungel	[e]	name, angel
/oh/	o, ou	[ɔː]*	bon, soule	[o]	bone, soul

*[ʊ] as in Modern English *full*; [æɪ] is a glide of the sounds indicated, with stress on the first element; the other vowels are lengthened counterparts (shown by : after the letter) of [e, o, u, æ, a, ɔ], the vowels of Modern English *day, bone, food, can, ox, thought*.

undertaken as a primarily linguistic procedure and is carried out thoroughly except when it seriously affects the aesthetic qualities of a construction (see, for example, 31.60, with footnote); it then becomes in effect a problem in emendation.

Emendation, by contrast, may be stipulated to consist of addition, deletion, or substitution with respect to the sequence of morphemes in a specified text. "Nou y may ȝef y wole" is altered to "Now I may if that you leste (33.23). Emendation is undertaken as a primarily textual or critical procedure to correct an obvious error in original transcription, improve the sense, restore a rhyme, or regularize a line. Most emendations are minor adjustments; several are modeled on readings in other copies or versions; and nearly all have been suggested by previous editors. Among the important emendations introduced here for the first time are changes for 32.18, 33.23, and 39.12 *(weild)*. One text (No. 19) has been virtually dismantled and reassembled. Except for established restorations and corrections and for a few regular replacements—*but* for *ac, wyth* for *mid*, and a few etymologically related modal verb forms—emendations are listed in footnotes.

The metrical features of a given text of Middle English lyric verse can be reconstructed consistently and in detail. But the procedures of reconstruction require complex analyses of spelling, dialect, date, variant texts (if any), and several other kinds of evidence. Whether final (spelled) *-e*, for instance, represents a syllable or not can sometimes be decided only tentatively, though at other times there is no doubt. During the period from which the poems were written down, the inflectional *-e* progressively lost syllabic status (hence losing inflectional function). Some poems occur in two or more texts of different dates and, therefore, show differences between metrical function implied by spelled *-e*; some individual texts are inconsistent in use of spelled *-e*. Even in principal words, historical sound changes have given rise to many instances in which metrical details implied by spelling in the manuscripts apparently differ from those of oral versions to which the written text is related. Two occurrences of the word rendered *fowel* throughout this book illustrate this point. In No. 2, line 2, the manuscript reads *fugheles;* in No. 27, line 3, the manuscript reads *foul.* In both poems, alternation of stressed and unstressed syllables is sufficiently prevalent to suggest that the word root in the first example should constitute one metrical stress and perhaps should be read as one syllable—

Wўth fówelĕs sóng

while the second perhaps should be read as two syllables—

Thĕ lítĕl fówĕl háth hĭr wýl.

General expectations of syllabic rhythm in these instances, then, are opposite to expectations based on original spelling.

While one may despair of being able unerringly to resolve Middle English lyric verse into syllables in order to infer meter —at least until he has studied the Middle English language extensively—the nonspecialist may yet take hope. Of course, the more accurately a reader can recognize syllable divisions in verses, the better he can read a poem. But most Middle English lyric verse is based on stress-rhythm rather than on syllable-rhythm. Even when successive lines of a poem regularly show, say, eight syllables alternating by degree of stress, it is the stress that establishes the rhythm. Very commonly, as it happens, stress occurs on two successive syllables and two or three unstressed syllables occur in sequence, and it is inappropriate to "explain" that a spondee, a trochee, an inversion, or what not has been substituted for an expected iamb. That a number of the lyrics are words of songs for dancing suggests that syllable-rhythm (in a language with fixed stress for words) is less important than stress-rhythm. The principal metrical feature of the poems, therefore, may be indicated by the following marking of passages in which the two lines just cited occur:

Mýrie it ís whil sómer y-lást
Wyth fówel-es sóng;
Bút now neígh-eth wýn-des blást
And wé-der stróng.

Bi-twén-e March and Á- per- íl
Whan spráy bi-gýnn-eth to sprýnge,
The lí-tel fówel háth hir wýl
Ón hir léde to sýnge.

In these examples, only stressed syllables are marked; equal spacing between stresses (on the page) symbolizes equal intervals between their occurrence when the lines are spoken. The number and timing of syllables not standing under stress vary. In the second example, from No. 27, -eth to (line 2) will be different from -tel (line 3), and both will differ from the timing of hir (lines 3 and 4). The final unstressed -e in sprynge, lede, synge will differ still further; in the first example, No. 2, timing of -er y- and whil (line 1) will necessarily be different, as will and and -der (line 4). (Adoption of fixed spelling of morphs and regularized morphology for the texts in this edition, while it changes the data upon which syllabic divisions can be made, hardly affects the nature of the evidence for metrical decisions; under stress-rhythm analysis, the poems will be nearly the same in normalized texts as in original texts.) In short, the nonspecialist can handle the matter of metrics satisfactorily and without essential error as soon as he develops a sensitivity to syllabic structure of Middle English words and attends to stress-rhythm of the verse. Because stress position in most Middle English words corresponds to stress position in their Modern English cognates, a reader can infer enough of the rhythm when he first reads a text to proceed quickly to a reasonably accurate metrical rendering of the poem.

Abbreviations of Titles

PREFACE

The purpose and editorial procedure of this book are explained in the Introduction. The acknowledgments may be stated briefly. To the editors, grammarians, lexicographers, and teachers whose publications and efforts have been drawn upon in preparing this volume is owed the measure of gratitude understood only by those who have edited centuries-old literary texts. Mr. G. M. Paul assisted with Latin translations. My wife has given encouragement and ever welcome assistance in proofreading.

    R. D. S.

CONTENTS

Texts of the Lyrics

A note on the glosses: In addition to translation glosses, equivalence glosses in Middle English have been included and appear in italic type following an = sign. Glossed words having special syntactic use can be identified by the *i.e.* that follows the bold-face glossed word.

1

Myrie songen the monkes binne⁺ Ely
Whan Cnut Kyng rewe⁺ ther-by:
Roweth, knightes, neer the lond
4 And here we thise monkes song.

Index 2164. Trinity Coll. Camb. MS. 1105. (J. E. Wells, *A Manual of the Writings in Middle English, 1050-1400*, p. 490.)
Unique text. *c.* 1150.

1. **binne** within
2. **rewe** rowed

2

Myrie it is whil somer ylast⁺
Wyth foweles song;
But now neigheth wyndes blast
4 And weder strong.
Ei! Ei! What, this nyght is long,
And I wyth⁺ wel muchel wrong
Sorwe and murne and faste.

Index 2163. Rawlinson MS. G. 22. (*EL XIII* No. 7.)
With music. Unique text. *c.* 1225.

1. **ylast** lasts, endures, continues
6. **wyth** because of, as a result of

3

Somer[+] is i-comen in,
Loude syng cuckow!
Groweth seed and bloweth[+] meed
4 And spryngeth the wode now.
Syng cuckow!
Ewe bleteth after lamb,
Loweth after calve cow;
8 Bullock sterteth,[+] bukke[+] farteth,—
Myrie syng cuckow!
Cuckow! Cuckow!
Wel syngest thou cuckow:
12 Ne swik[+] thou nevere now.
Syng cuckow, now, syng cuckow!
Syng cuckow, syng cuckow, now!

Index 3223. MS. Harley 978. (*EL XIII* No. 6.)
With music. Unique text, 1230-1240. *c.* 1225.

1. **somer** spring
3. **bloweth** blows, bursts into flower, blooms
8. **sterteth** starts, leaps; **bukke** buck, stag
12. **swik** cease, stop

4

Now goth sonne under wode,—
Me reweth, Marie, thy faire rode.[+]
Now goth sonne under tree,—
4 Me reweth, Marie, thy sone and thee.

Index 2320. Bodleian MS. Arch. Selden, supra 74. (*EL XIII* No. 1.)
Contained in 36 MSS. in French, Latin, and English. *c.* 1240.

2. **rode** face, visage

5

Man may longe lyves[+] wene,[+]
  But ofte him lieth the wrench;[+]
Faire weder wendeth ofte into reyn
4   And ferly maketh his blench.[+]
  Ther-fore, man, thou thee bithenk,—
Al shal falewe[+] the grene.
Weylawey! nis kyng ne quene
8   That ne shal drynke of Dethes drench.[+]
Man, er thou falle offe thy bench,
Thy synne a-quench.

Ne may strong ne stark ne kene
12   A-glye Dethes wither-clench;[+]
Yong ne old, bright ne shene,
  Alle he riveth in his strengthe.
Fous and ferly[+] is the wrench,
16 Ne may him no man ther-toyeins—

Index 2070. Maidstone MS. A. 13, Laud Misc. 471. (*EL XIII* 10A, 10B.)

Reconstructed from texts cited, with variants, as noted, from Cotton MS. Caligula A. ix and Jesus Coll. Oxf. MS. 29 (*OEM* XX). Four full texts. With music. *c.* 1250.

1. **lyves** life. *Wene* here has its object in the genitive case. The line means: "Man may expect to have a long life."
2. **wrench** deception; sudden turning (of affairs)
4. **ferly maketh his blench** suddenly, wonderfully plays his trick
6. **falewe** wither, fade
8. **drench** = *drynke*, draught
12. **A-glye Dethes wither-clench** escape Death's hostile grasp
15. **Fous and ferly** ready and sudden, eager and terrible

6

Weylawey! wepyng ne bene,[+]
  Mede, list,[+] ne leches drench.
  Man, lat synne and lustes stench;
20   Wel do, wel thenk.

Do by Salomones rede,
  Man, and so thou shalt wel do;
Do as he thee taughte and seyde
24   What thyn endyng thee bryngeth to,
  Ne shalt thou nevere mys-do.
Sore thou myghte thee adrede,
Weylawey! swich weneth wel lede
28   Long lyf and blisse under-fo;[+]
  But Deeth luteth in his sho[+]
  To him for-do.[+]

Man, why n'iltow thee biknowe?
32   Man, why n'iltow thee bisee?
Of filthe thou art issue—
  Wormes mete thou shalt be.
Heer navest[+] thou blisse dayes three,
36 But al thy lyf thou dreyest[+] in wo.
Weylawey! Deeth thee shal doun throwe
  Ther[+] thou wenest heighe stye;[+]
  In wo shal thy wele ende,
40   In wop[+] thy glee.

17. **bene** prayer, supplication
18. **list** craft, cunning
28. **under-fo** receive
29. **luteth in his sho** lurks in his shoe. *But* supplied (for *ac*) from Cotton Caligula and Jesus Coll. Oxf. MSS.
30. **for-do** destroy
35. **navest** = *ne havest, ne hast*
36. **dreyest** endure, suffer
38. **ther** i.e., there where; **stye** climb, ascend
40. **wop** lamentation, weeping

World and wele thee biswiketh;+
  Y-wis, they ben thy fo!
If the world wyth wele thee sliketh,+
44   That is for to do thee wo.
  Ther-fore lat lust over-go,
Man, and eft it thee liketh.
Weylawey! sore he him wiketh+
48   That in oon stounde or two
  Werketh him pyne evermo.
  Ne do thou so!

---

41. **biswiketh** deceives
43. **sliketh** flatters
47. **wiketh** yields, fails
48. *That* replacing *thar/thanne*, from the other MSS.

6

If man him bithoghte
Inwardly⁺ and ofte
How hard is the fore⁺
4 From bed to floor,
How reweful is the flitte⁺
From floor to pitte,⁺
From pitte to pyne
8 That nevere shal fyne,⁺—
I wene non synne
Sholde his herte wynne.

Index 1422. Arundel MS. 292. (*EL XIII* No. 13.)
Many other texts, variants, versions; as mural inscription and as
  tombstone inscription: 13th to 16th centuries. *c.* 1250.

2. **inwardly** earnestly; MS. *inderlike*
3. **fore** going, journey
5. **flitte** departing, removal
6. **pitte** pit, grave
8. **fyne** end, finish

7

Have oon god in worshipe,
Ne nem[+] thou his name in idelshipe,[+]
Wite wel thyn holy-day,
4   Fader and moder worship ay;
Loke that thou ne slee no man,
Ne synne by non womman;
Fals oth that thou ne swere,
8   Fals witnesse that thou ne bere;
Non mannes wyf after longe,
Ne of his thyng to han wyth wronge.[+]

Thise ben Goddes bodes[+] ten
12   That shullen kepen alle men:
They that nollen[+] hem ykepe,
They shullen into helle depe;
They that kepen hem aright,
16   They shullen into hevene bright.

Index 1129. Trinity Coll. Camb. MS. 323. (*EL XIII* No. 23.)
Seven versions, largely independent of each other. *c.* 1250.

2. **nem** call, name; **idelshipe** idleness, vain
10. **wyth wronge** wrongfully
11. **bodes** commands, commandments
13. **nollen** = *ne wollen*

8

Sey me, wight in the broom,[+]
Teche me how I shal don
That myn housebonde
4 Me loven wolde.

"Hold thy tonge stille
And have al thy wylle."

Index 3078. Trinity Coll. Camb. MS. 323. (*EL XIII* No. 21.)
One other text. *c.* 1250.

1. **broom** broom, brushwood

9

Whan the turf is thy tour
And thy put+ is thy bour,
Thy fel+ and thy white throte
4 Shullen wormes to note.+
What helpeth thee than
Al the worlde wenne?+

Index 4044. Trinity Coll. Camb. MS. 323. (*EL XIII* No. 30.)
Unique text; directly translated from Latin verses. *c.* 1250.

2. **put** = *pit*, i.e., grave
3. **fel** skin
4. **Shullen wormes to note** shall worms (have) for their use (or purpose)
6. **worlde wenne** joys, pleasures of the world; (?) to win the world

10

Now thise foweles syngen and maken her blisse,
And that gras up thryngeth and leveth the rys;+
Of oon I wyl synge that is makeles,
4   The kyng of alle kynges to moder He hire ches.+

She is wythouten synne and wythouten hore,+
I-comen of kynges kyn of Jesses more;+
The lord of mankynde of hire was i-born
8   To brynge us out of synne, elles we weren forlorn.

Gabriel hire grette and seyde hire, "Ave!
Marie ful of grace, oure Lord be wyth thee;
The fruyt of thy womb i-blessed moot it be.
12   Thou shalt gon wyth childe, for sothe+ I seye it thee."

Whan that gretyng that aungel hadde i-broght,
She gan to bithenke and meinde+ hir thoght;
She seyde to the aungel, "How may tiden+ this?
16   Of mannes y-mone+ not+ I noght, y-wis."

Index 2366. Trinity Coll. Camb. MS. 323. (*EL XIII* No. 31.)
Unique text. *c.* 1250.

2. **leveth the rys** the small branch (of a bush) puts forth leaves
4. **ches** chose
5. **hore** stain, defilement
6. **more** stock, root
12. **for sothe** forsooth, for truth
13. *Whan* replaces MS. *and*
14. **meinde** mingled, disturbed
15. **tiden** betide, come to pass
16. **y-mone** company, intercourse; **not** = *ne wot* know not

Mayden she was wyth childe and mayden heer-biforn,
And mayden er sith-that hir child was i-born;
Mayden and moder was nevere non womman but she:
20 Wel myghte she berere of Goddes sone be.

I-blessed be that swete child and the moder eke,
And the swete brest that hir sone seek;+
I-heried be the tyme that swich child was i-born,
24 That lesed+ al of pyne that erre+ was forlorn.

19. *was* for MS. *nas*
22. **seek** sucked
24. **lesed** loosed, released, delivered; **erre** before, formerly

11

Of oon that is so faire and bright,
   Velud maris stella,[+]
Brighter thanne the dayes light,
4   *Parens et puella:*
I crie to thee, thou see to me.
Lady, preye thy Sone for me,
   Tam pia,
8 That I moot come to thee,
   Maria.

Of care counseil[+] thou art best;
   Felix fecundata.
12 Of alle wery thou art reste,
   Mater honorata.
Biseech thou Him wyth mylde mood,
That for us alle shedde his blood
16   *In cruce,*
That we mote come to Him
   In luce.

Index 2645. Egerton MS. 613, and Trinity Coll. Camb. MS 323.
   (*EL XIII* 17A, 17B.)
The text here follows the Egerton MS. except as noted. *c.* 1250.

2. **Velud maris stella** as the star of the sea. (All remaining Latin lines
   are glossed below without notice within the text of the poem.)
4. **Parens et puella** i.e., *moder and mayden*
7. **Tam pia** you who are so gracious
9. **Maria** Mary
10. **counseil** consolation
11. **Felix fecundata** i.e., blessed is the fruit of thy womb
13. **Mater honorata** mother (who is) honored
14. *thou* not in Egerton MS.
16. **In cruce** on the cross
18. **In luce** in the light

Al this world was forlorn
20   *Eve peccatrice,*
Til oure Lord was i-born
   De te genetrice.
Wyth *Ave* it went awey
24 Thester+ nyght and cam the day
   Salutis;
The welle spryngeth out of thee
   Virtutis.

28 Lady, flour of alle thyng,
   Rosa sine spina,
Thou bare Jhesu, hevenes kyng
   Gratia divina.
32 Of alle thou berest the pris,
Lady, quene of paradys,
   Electa,
Moder mylde and mayden eke
36   *Effecta.*

20. **Eva peccatrice** through Eve (being) a sinner; because Eve sinned
22. **De te genetrice** i.e., from you His mother
24. **Thester** dark; *cam,* based on T.C.C. MS., replaces Egerton MS. *comet*
25. **Salutis** of safety, of salvation
27. **Virtutis** of virtue
29. **Rosa sine spina** rose without thorn
31. **Gratia divina** by divine grace
34. **Electa** elected, the elected one
35. *Moder mylde and mayden eke* follows T.C.C. MS., replacing Egerton MS. *Mayde milde Moder es.*
36. **Effecta** created

Wel He wot He is thy sone
Ventre quem portasti;
He wyl not werne⁺ thee thy boon
40   *Parvum quem lactasti.*
So hende and so good He is,
He hath broght us alle to blisse
Superni,
44   That hath i-dut⁺ the foule put⁺
Inferni.

38. **Ventre quem portasti** whom you carried in your belly
39. **werne** refuse
40. **Parvum quem lactasti** whom you suckled when small
42. *alle*, from T.C.C. MS., not in Egerton MS.
43. **Superni** on high
44. **i-dut** closed, shut; **put** = *pit* grave
45. **Inferni** below

12

On hire is al my lyf ylong⁺
Of whom I wylle synge,
And herien hire ther-among⁺
4   That gan us boot⁺ brynge
Of helle-pyne that is strong,
And broghte us blisse that is long,
Al thurgh hir childyng.⁺
8   I bidde hire in my song
She yeve us good endyng,
Thogh we don wrong.

Al this world shal a-go⁺
12   Wyth sorwe and wyth sore;⁺
And al this blisse we shullen forgo,
Ne of-thinken⁺ it us so sore: ⁺
This world nis but oure fo.

Index 2687. Trinity Coll. Camb. MS. 323, with variants based on
(C) Cotton MS. Caligula A. ix; (R) Royal MS. 2.F.viii; (J)
Jesus Coll. Oxf. MS. 29. (*EL XIII* No. 32A, 32B, 32C, and
OEM No. XXI.)
Four texts, with different order of stanzas. *c.* 1250.

1. **ylong** dependent
3. **ther-among** i.e., in the course of my singing; *hire* from C, R, J, for
   MS. *him*
4. **boot** salvation, redress
6. *so* omitted before *long*, as in C, R, J
7. **childyng** child-bearing
8. *I* and *my*, from C, R, J, for MS. *We* and *ure*
11. **a-go** pass away (utterly); *hid* (it) omitted before *shal*, as in C, R, J
12. **sore** (noun) pain, grief, suffering
13. *we shullen* from C, R, J, for MS. *ic mot*
14. **Ne of-thinken . . . us** we should not regret, grieve about, repent;
    sore (adverb); *it, us* from C, R, J, for MS. *me*

16   Ther-fore I wyl hennes go
      And lernen Goddes lore;
      This worldes blisse nis worth a slo⁺—
      I bidde, God, thyn ore,
20   Now and evermore.

      To long I have sot⁺ i-be;
      Ful sore I me adrede;⁺
      I-loved I have gamen and glee
24   And evere faire wede.⁺
      Al that nis noght, ful wel I see,
      Ther-fore I wyl hem flee
      And lete myn sot-hede.⁺
28   I bidde hire me to see⁺
      That can wisse and rede,⁺
      That is so free.

      Thou art hele and lyf and light
32   And helpest al mankynne;
      Thou us hast ful wel i-dight,
      Thou yafe us wele and wynne.
      Thou broghtest day and Eve nyght;
36   She broghte wo, thou broghtest right;

18. **slo** sloe, blackthorn berry
21. **sot** foolish
22. **me adrede** (reflexive) I am afraid
24. **wede** clothing, garments
26. *I wyl hem*, based on R, for MS. *we sulin ur sunnis*
27. **sot-hede** foolishness, folly; *lete myn*, based on R, for MS. *ure*
28. **see** watch over, protect; *I* and *me*, based on C and R, for MS. *we* and *us*
29. **wisse and rede** direct, guide and counsel
31. *Thou*, here and subsequently, from C, R, J, for MS. *Heo/Ho*

Thou almesse⁺ and she synne.
Bisee⁺ to me, lady brighte,
Whan I shal wende henne⁺—
40 Ful wel thou myghte.

Agulte⁺ I have, weylawey!
Synful I am and wrecche!
Thou do me mercy, swete lady,
44 Er deeth me hennes fecche.
Yef me thy love, I am redy,
Lat me lyve and amendy⁺
That fendes me ne lette;⁺
48 For my synnes I am sory,
Of my lyf I ne recche.⁺
Lady, mercy! Amen.

---

37. **almesse** charity, charitable gifts
38. **Bisee** give heed to, attend to; *Bisee to me*, based on C, R, J, for MS. *þu do us merci*
39. **wende henne** = *wende hennes*, i.e., die; *I shal*, from C, R, J, for MS. *we sulin*
41. **Agulte** offended, been guilty, been sinful
43. *swete lady*, from R, for MS. *lauedi brit*
46. **amendy** = *amende*
47. **lette** hinder, cut off
49. **recche** care for, have regard for

13

Whoso saw on rode
Jhesus his lemman,—
Sory stood him by wepynge
4 Seint Marie and Seint John,—
His hed him al aboute
Wyth thornes i-priked,
His faire hondes and his faire feet
8 Wyth nayles i-stiked,
His rigge+ wyth yerdes+ swongen,
His side wyth spere i-wounded—
Al for synne of man:
12 Sore he may wepe
And bittre teres lete,
Man that of love can.

Index 4141. Trinity Coll. Camb. MS. 323. (*EL XIII* No. 34.)
Unique text, *c.* 1250, but see other versions following.

9. **rigge** back; **yerdes** rods

14

Whan I see on rode i-don
Jhesus my lemman,
And by him stonden
4 Marie and Iohan,
His herte depe i-stongen,
His body wyth scourge i-swongen
For the synne of man:
8 Ethe⁺ I may wepe
And salte teres lete
If I of love can.

14B

Whan I see on rode
Jhesu my lemman,
And biside him stonden
4 Marie and Iohan,
And his rigge⁺ i-swongen,
And his side i-stongen
For the love of man:
8 Wel owe I to wepe
And synnes forlete,
If I of love can,
If I of love can,
12 If I of love can.

Index 3965. (A) St. John's Coll. Camb. MS. 15; *Index* 3964. (B)
   Royal MS. 12. E. i. (*EL XIII* No. 35A, 35B.)
Unique versions. Early 14th century.

A. 6. *wyth* for MS. *þis*
   8. **ethe** easily, readily

B. 5. **rigge** back

15

Whan I on the rode see
Faste nayled to the tree
 Jhesu my lemman,
4 I-bounde blak[+] and blody,
And his moder stonde him by
 Wepyng and Iohan;

His bak wyth scourge i-swongen,
8 His side depe i-stongen
 For synne and love of man:
Wel oghte I synne lete
And neb[+] wyth teres wete,
12 If I of love can.

Index 3961. MS. Bodleian 57. (*EL XIII* No. 36.)
Unique version. *c.* 1300.

4. **blak** pale
11. **neb** face

16

When I thenke on the rode
Wher-upon thou stood,
   Swete Jhesu my lemman;
4 How by thee was stondyng
Thy moder wepyng
   And thy disciple Seint Iohan;
How thy rigge[+] was i-swongen,
8 And thy side thurgh-stongen
   For the gilt of man;
How thy feet y-bledden,
And thyne hondes y-spredden
12   That they myghten telle[+] thy bon;
How the stones to-breken,[+]
The dede arisen and speken,
   The sonne wex al wan:
16 No sely[+] thogh I wepe
And my synnes bete[+]
   If I love wel can.

Index 3968. MS. Ashmole 360. (*EL XIII* No. 37.)
Unique version. 13th century.

7. **rigge** back
12. **telle** count
13. **to-breken** broke to pieces
16. **sely** wonder, marvel
17. **bete** amend, make amends for

17

Foweles in the frith,+
The fisshes in the flood,
And I mon+ waxe wood:
4   Muche sorwe I walke wyth
For best+ of bon and blood.

Index 864. Bodleian MS. Douce 139. (*EL XIII* No. 8.)
With music. Unique text. *c.* 1270.

1. **frith** woodland, forest
3. **mon** must
5. **best** i.e., the best (person)

18

Wher beth they biforn us weren,
Houndes ladden and haukes beren
And hadden feeld and wode?
4 The riche ladies in her bour
That werede gold in her tresour,+
Wyth her brighte rode?+

They eten and dronken and maden hem glad—
8 Her lyf was al wyth gamen i-lad;
Men kneleden hem biforn;
They beren hem wel swithe heighe,
And, in a twynkelyng of an eye,
12 Her soules weren forlorn.

Wher is that laughyng and that song,
That trailyng+ and that proude yong,+
Tho haukes and tho houndes?
16 Al that joye is went+ awey—
That wele is comen to weylawey,
To many harde stoundes.

Index 3310. MS. Digby 86. (*EL XIII* No. 48.)
Also in Vernon MS., MS. Harley 2253, and MS. Laud 108, all
three in *The Minor Poems of the Vernon MS*, ed. F. J. Furnivall, EETS OS. 117. *c.* 1270.

5. **tresour** head-dress
6. **rode** face, countenance
7. *They* supplied from the other MSS.
14. **trailyng** long, trailing garments; **yong** walk, gait
16. **went** turned, gone

Her paradys they nomen+ heer,
20 And now they liggen+ in helle y-fere;+
The fyr it brenneth evere.
Long is ay and long is o,
Long is wei and long is wo—
24 Thennes ne comen they nevere.

Drey+ heer, man, than if thou wylt
A litel pyne that me thee bit;+
Wythdraw thyne eses+ ofte.
28 Thogh thy pyne be unrede,+
And+ thou thenke on thy mede
It shal thee thynken softe.

If that feend, that foule thyng,
32 Thurgh wikked roun,+ thurgh fals eggyng,
Nethere+ thee hath i-cast,
Up and be good champioun!
Stond, ne fal namore adoun
36 For a litel blast!

Thou tak the rode to thy staf,
And thenk on him that ther-on yaf
His lyf that was so leef.

19. **nomen** took, seized
20. **liggen** lie; **y-fere** together, in company
25. **Drey** endure, suffer
26. **me thee bit** one (anyone) bids you; men bid you
27. **eses** comforts
28. **unrede** severe
29. **and** if
32. **roun** advice
33. **nethere** down, downward

40 He it yaf for thee, thou yeld it him: +
Ayeins his fo that staf thou nim+
And wrek+ him of that theef.

Of right bileve, thou nim that sheeld
44 The whiles that thou best in that feeld,
Thyn hond to strengthen fond! +
And keep thy fo wyth staves ord, +
And do that traytour seyn that word: +
48 Biget that myrie lond!

Ther-inne is day wythouten nyght,
Wythouten ende strengthe and myght,
And wreche+ of every fo;
52 Wyth God him-selve eche+ lyf,
And pees and reste wythouten strif—
Wele wythouten wo.

Mayden moder, hevenes quene,
56 Thou myghte and canst and owest to ben
Oure sheeld ayeins the feend.
Help us synnes for-to fleen,
That we mote thy sone seen
60 In joye wythouten ende. Amen.

40. **thou yeld it him** repay him for it
41. **nim** seize, take
42. **wrek** avenge
45. **fond** try, attempt
46. **ord** point (?); the sense of this line is "meet thy foe with opposition."
47. **word**, *i.e.*, word of surrender
51. **wreche** vengeance
52. **eche** eternal, everlasting

19

"Stond wel, Moder, under rode,
Bihold thy child wyth gladde mood;
Blithe, Moder, myghtestow be."
4   "Sone, how may I blithe stonde?
I see thy feet, I see thyne honde+
Nayled to the harde tree."

"Moder, do wey thy wepyng,
8   I thole this deeth for mannes thyng;
For my gilt ne thole I non."
"Sone, I fele the dethes stounde;
That swerd is at myn hertes grounde,
12   That me bihete Simeon."

"Moder, rewe upon thy bern;+
Thou wassh awey the blody teren:+
It doth me worse thanne my deeth."

Index 3211. MS. Digby 86. (*EL XIII* No. 49A.)
With variants from (R) Royal MS. 12.E.i, with music (*EL XIII* No. 49B); (H) MS. Harley 2253 (*HL* No. 20); and (J) St. John's Coll. Camb. MS. 111, with music (*EL XIII* pp. 203-204). Four full versions. *c.* 1270.

3. MS. *Moder bliþe;* R, H, J *Bliþe moder.*
5. **honde** = *hondes.* Line based on R and H, for MS. *Ich se þine fet and þine honde.*
8. Line based on R, for MS. *Ich þolie deþ for monnes kuinde.*
13. **bern** son. Line based on R, for MS. *Moder, do wei þine teres.*
14. **teren** = *teres.* Line based on R and H, for MS. *þou wiþ awey þe blodi teres.*

16   "Sone, how myghte I teres werne?[+]
     I see thy blody woundes erne[+]
     From thyn herte to my feet."

     "Moder, now I may thee seye,
20   Bettre is that ich oone deye
     Thanne al mankynde to helle go."
     "Sone, I see thy body i-swongen—
     Thy brest, thyne honde, thy feet thurgh-stongen:
24   No sely[+] is thogh me be wo."

     "Moder, if I thee durste telle,
     If I ne deye thou gost to helle;
     I thole this deeth for mannes sake."
28   "Sone, thou best so meke and mynde,[+]
     Ne wyte[+] me noght—it is my kynde
     That I for thee this sorwe make."

     "Moder, mercy! lat me deye
32   And Adam out of helle beye,
     And al mankynde that is forlorn."
     "Sone, what shal me to rede?
     Thy pyne pyneth me to dede:[+]
36   Lat me deye thee biforn."

16. **werne** restrain
17. **erne** run, flow
18. *my feet,* based on R and H, for MS. *þy fot.*
23-24. Based on R, for MS. *þine honde, þine fet, þi bodi I-stounge;* / *Hit nis no wonder þey me be wo.*
24. **sely** wonder, marvel
27. *this* supplied from R.
28-30. Lines based on R and H, for MS. *Sone, þou me bi-hest so milde;* / *I-comen hit is of monnes kuinde* / *þat ich sike and serewe make.*
28. **mynde** mindful, thoughtful
29. **wyte** blame
33. *al* supplied from R.
34-35. Lines based on R and H, for MS. *Sone, wat sal me þe stounde?* / *þine pinen me bringeþ to þe grounde.* **dede** dead

"Moder, now thou myghte wel lernen
What pyne tholen that children beren,
What sorwe han that child forgon."+
40 "Sone, I wot I may thee telle
But it be the pyne of helle;
Of more pyn ne wot I non."

"Moder, rewe of modres care
44 Now thou wost of modres fare,+
Thogh thou be clene mayden-man."+
"Sone, thou helpest at the nede
Alle tho that to thee grede,+
48 Mayden, wyfe, and fole+ womman."

"Moder, I may no lenger dwelle—
The tyme is comen I shal to helle:
The thridde day I rise upon."
52 "Sone, I wyl wyth thee founden,+
I deye y-wis of thyne wounden;+
So reweful deeth was nevere non."

37-39. Lines based on R and H, for MS. *Swete moder, nou þou fondest /
Of mi pine, þer þou stondest; / Wiþ-houte mi pine nere no mon.*
39. **forgon** relinquish, forego, lose
43-48. Lines based on R, for MS. *Moder, of moder þus I fare. / Nou þou
wost wimmanes kare, / þou art clene mayden on. / Sone, þou helpest
alle nede, / Alle þo þat to þe wille grede, / May and wif and fowel
wimmon.*
44. **fare** lot, fate
45. **mayden-man** a maiden, virgin
47. **grede** call out, pray, cry
48. **fole** foolish
50. *shal* from H, for MS. *go*
51-54. Lines based on R, for MS. *I þolie þis for þine sake. / Sone, I-wis
I wille founde, / I deye almest, I falle to grounde, / So serwful deþ
nes never non.*
52. **founden** depart, leave, go away
53. **wounden** = *woundes*

31

Whan he ros than fil hir sorwe;
56 The blisse sprong the thridde morwe.
Blithe moder were thou tho!
Lady, for that ilke blisse,
Biseech thy Sone oure synnes lisse; +
60 Thou be oure sheeld ayeins oure fo.

Blessed be thou, quene of hevene!
Bryng us out of helle levene +
Thurgh thy dere sones myght.
64 Moder, for that heighe blood
That He shedde upon the rode,
Leed us into hevenes light.

55-66. Based on R and H; absent in MS. Digby 86.
59. **synnes lisse** remission of sins
62. **helle levene** the lightning, flame, of hell

20

Ne hath my soule but fyr and yse
And the licame⁺ erthe and tree:
Bidde we alle the heighe kyng
4   That welde⁺ shal the laste doom
That he us lete that ilke thyng,
That we mowen his wylle don;
He us skere of the tithyng⁺
8   That synfulle shullen an-underfon,⁺
Whan deeth hem ledeth to the myrthe⁺
That nevere ne beth undon.   Amen.

———. Jesus Coll. Oxf. MS. 29. (*OEM* No. XII.) *c*. 1275.

2. **licame** body
4. **welde** wield, rule over
7. **skere of the tithyng** free (or excuse) from the wages (reward)
8. **an-underfon** receive
9. **myrthe** mirth, joys (obviously ironic)

33

21

Whan I thenke thynges three
Ne may I nevere blithe be:
That oon is that I shal awey;
4   That other is I ne wot which day;
The thridde is my moste care—
I ne wot whider I shal fare.

Index 3969. New Coll. Oxf. MS. 88 and Arundel MS. 292. (*EL
XIII* No. 12A, 12B.)
Three other texts; also, other versions. *c.* 1300.

22

Lord, thou clepedest me
And I noght ne answerde thee
But wordes slowe and slepy:
4   "Thole yet! Thole a litel!"
But "yet" and "yet" was endeles,
And "thole a litel" a long weye is.

Index 1978. New Coll. Oxf. MS. 88. (*RL XIV* No. 5.)
Unique text. *c.* 1300.

23

Wel, who shal thise hornes blowe
　　Holy Rode thy day?[+]
Now is he deed and lieth lowe
4　　Was wont to blowe hem ay.

Index 3894. Lansdowne MS. 207(e). (*EMET* p. 118.)
After 1280.

2. **Holy Rode thy day** Holy Cross Day (September 14)

24

Myrie a tyme I telle in May
　　Whan brighte blosmes breken[+] on tree;
This foweles syngen nyght and day:
4　　In ilke greyn[+] is gamen and glee.

Index 2162. Pembroke Coll. Camb. MS. 258. (*SL XIV-XV* No.
　141.)
Unique text. *c.* 1300.

2. **breken** burst into flower
4. **ilke greyn** each green, grassy spot

25

Now spryngeth the spray,
Al for love I am so sik
That slepen I ne may.

As I me rod this endre day
   On my pleyinge,
Saw I wher a litel may
4   Bigan to synge:
"The clot him clynge! +
Wei is him+ in love-longynge
   Shal lyven ay:
8   Now spryngeth the spray,
     Al for love I am so sik
     That slepen I ne may."

Soon+ I herde that myrie note
12   Thider I drough;
I fond hire in an herber swote+
   Under a bough,
   Wyth joye ynough.
16 Soon I axed: "Thou myrie may,
   Why syngestow ay
    'Now spryngeth the spray,
    Al for love I am so sik
20   That slepen I ne may?' "

Index 360. Lincoln's Inn MS. Hale 135. (*EL XIII* No. 62.)
Unique text. (See Introduction, p. xv.) *c.* 1300.

5. **The clot him clynge** may the clay cling to him, i.e., would he were
   dead
6. **Wei is him** woe be to (or there is woe for) him who
11. **Soon** as soon as
13. **swote** = *swete* pleasant

Than answerde that mayden swote
  Wyth wordes fewe:
"My lemman me haveth bihote
24   Of love trewe;
  He chaungeth anew.
If I may, it shal him rewe
  By this day."
28   *Now spryngeth the spray,*
      Al for love I am so sik
      That slepen I ne may.

26

Erthe took of erthe, erthe wyth wogh; [+]
Erthe other erthe to the erthe drough; [+]
Erthe leyde erthe in erthen through: [+]
4 Than hadde erthe of erthe erthe ynough.

Index 3939. MS. Harley 2253. (*EL XIII* No. 73.)
Many variants, versions, and expansions. *c.* 1320.

1. **wogh** wrong, harm
2. **drough** drew, added
3. **through** coffin, grave

27

Bitwene March and Aperil,
Whan spray bigynneth to sprynge,
The litel fowel hath hir wyl
4 On hir lede⁺ to synge.
I lyve in love-longynge
For semlokest⁺ of alle thyng;
She may me blisse brynge:
8 I am in hir baundoun.⁺
    An hende hap I have i-hent,⁺
    I wot from hevene it is me sent;—
    From alle wommen my love is lent⁺
12   And light on Alysoun.

On hewe hir heer is faire ynough,
Hir browes broune, hir eyen blake,
Wyth lufsom chere she on me lough,⁺
16 Wyth myddel smal and wel i-mak.

Index 515. MS. Harley 2253. (*EL XIII* No. 77.)
Unique text. *c*. 1320.

4. **lede** language
6. **semlokest** seemliest, most fair
8. **baundoun** power, control, i.e., at her disposal
9. **An hende hap I have i-hent** I have received (obtained) a gracious fortune; I have got a piece of good luck
11. **lent** taken away, gone
14. *browes, eyen* are given plural inflexions here, for plural substantives in MS. *browe and eȝe.*
15. **Wyth lufsom chere she on me lough** with a lovely face she smiled on me

But she me wol to hire take
For-to ben hir owene make,
Longe to lyve I wyl forsake
20 And feye+ falle adoun.
    An hende hap I have i-hent,
    I wot from hevene it is me sent;—
    From alle wommen my love is lent
24   And light on Alysoun.

Nyghtes whan I wende+ and wake—
For-thy myne wonges+ waxen wan;
Lady, al for thy sake
28 Longyng is i-lent+ me on.
    In world nis non so witter+ man
    That al hir bountee+ telle can:
    Hir swire+ is whiter thanne the swan,
32 And fairest+ may in toun.
    An hende hap I have i-hent,
    I wot from hevene it is me sent;—
    From alle wommen my love is lent
36   And light on Alysoun.

20. **feye** doomed (to die)
25. **wende** turn (and toss)
26. **wonges** cheeks
28. **i-lent** come upon
29. **witter** wise
30. **bountee** excellence, virtue
31. **swire** neck
32. **fairest** (she is the) fairest

I am for wowyng al forwake, +
Wery as water in wore; +
Lest any reve me my make
40 I have i-yerned yore.
Bettre is tholen while sore
Thanne murnen evermore.
Geynest under gore, +
44 Herkne to my roun: +
An hende hap I have i-hent,
I wot from hevene it is me sent;—
From alle wommen my love is lent
48 And light on Alysoun.

---

37. **forwake** overwatched, worn out with lying awake
38. **wore** troubled pool (?); *so* for MS. *as*
43. **Gaynest under gore** kindest in gown, i.e., of all women, of any alive
44. **roun** speech

28

Lenten[+] is comen wyth love to toun—
Wyth blosmes and wyth briddes roun[+]—
   That al this blisse bryngeth;
4 Dayesyes in thise dales,
Notes swete of nyghtengales—
   Ech fowel song syngeth.
The thrustelcok him threteth[+] oo;
8 Awey is here wynter wo
   Whan woderove[+] spryngeth.
Thise foweles syngen ferly fele[+]
And wlyten[+] on her wynne wele[+]
12   That al the wode ryngeth.

The rose raileth hire rode,[+]
The leves on the lighte wode
   Waxen al wyth wylle;
16 The mone mandeth hire blee,[+]
The lilye is lufsom to see,
   The fenel and the fille.

Index 1861. MS. Harley 2253. (*EL XIII* No. 81.)
Unique text. *c.* 1320.

1. **lenten** spring
2. **roun** song
7. **threteth** contends, chides
9. **woderove** woodruff
10. **ferly fele** wondrously many
11. **wlyten** pipe, warble; **wynne wele** (for MS. *wynter wele*) wealth of joy
13. **raileth hire rode** puts on her rosy hue
16. **mandeth hire blee** sends forth her light, radiance

Wowen thise wilde drakes;
20   Miles myrien+ here makes,
    As streem that striketh stille.+
Mody meneth,+ so doth mo;+
I wot I am oon of tho,
24   For love that liketh ille.

The mone mandeth hire light,
So doth the seemly sonne bright,
    Whan briddes syngen breme;+
28   Dewes donken+ thise dounes,
Deres wyth her derne rounes
    Domes for-to deme.+
Wormes wowen under cloude,+
32   Wommen waxen wonder proude,
    So wel it wol hem seme.+
If me shal wante wylle of oon
This wynne wele I wol forgon
36   And wyght+ in wode be fleme.+

---

20. **miles myrien** animals (?) gladden
21. **striketh stille** flows softly, quietly
22. **mody meneth** the spirited man laments (complains); **mo** more, i.e., others
27. **breme** clearly, loudly
28. **donken** moisten, dampen
29-30. **Deres wyth her derne rounes / Domes for-to deme** Animals with their cries, unmeaning to us, whereby they converse. (See Kenneth Sisam, ed., *Fourteenth Century Verse and Prose*, p. 256.)
31. **cloude** earth, ground
33. **seme** befit, beseem
36. **wyght** quickly; **fleme** fugitive

29

Blow, Northren Wynd,
Send thou me my swetyng!
Blow, Northren Wynd,
Blow, blow, blow!

I wot a burde in boure bright
That fully seemly is on sight,
Menskful[+] mayden of myght,
4　Faire and free to fonde;[+]
In al this worthly won[+]
A burde of blood and of bon
Nevere yet I niste non[+]
8　Lufsomer in londe.

Wyth lokkes leefly[+] and longe,
Wyth frount[+] and face faire to fonde,
Wyth myrthes many moot she monge,[+]
12　That brid so brem[+] in boure;
Wyth lufsom eye greet and good
Wyth browes blisful under hood—
He that reste him on the rode,
16　That leefly lyf honoure!

Index 1395. MS Harley 2253. (*EL XIII* No. 83.)
Unique text. *c.* 1320.

3. **Menskful** noble, honorable, gracious
4. **fonde** examine; try, test
5. **worthly won** goodly country
7. **I niste non** (**niste** = *ne wiste*) have I known one
9. **leefly** lovable, delightful, beautiful
10. **frount** forehead
11. **monge** mingle with, i.e., be compared to
12. **brem** bright, splendid

Hir lere lumeth⁺ lighte
As a lanterne a-nyghte,
Hir blee bliketh⁺ so brighte
20 So faire she is and fyne;
A swetely swire⁺ she hath to holde,
Wyth armes, shuldres as man wolde,
Any fyngres faire for-to folde—
24 God wolde she were myn!

Myddel she hath menskful smal,⁺
Hir lovely chere as cristal,
Thighes, legges, feet, and al
28 I-wroght was of the best;
A lufsom lady lasteles⁺
That swetyng is and evere was—
A bettre burde nevere nas
32 I-heried wyth the best.

She is dereworthe⁺ in day,
Gracious, stout, and gay,
Gentil, joly so the jay,
36 Worthly⁺ whan she waketh;
Mayden muriest of mouth,
By est, by west, by north and south
Ther nis fiele⁺ ne crouth⁺
40 That swiche myrthes maketh.

17. **lere lumeth** countenance, complexion gleams
19. **blee bliketh** face shines, glistens
21. **swire** neck
25. **menskful smal** gracefully slender
29. **lasteles** faultless
33. **dereworthe** excellent, beloved
36. **worthly** excellent, worthy
39. **fiele, crouth** stringed musical instruments

44

She is coral of goodnesse,
She is ruby of rightfulnesse,
She is cristal of clennesse,
44 And baner of bealtee;+
She is lilye of largesse,
She is pervynke+ of prowesse,
She is solsecle+ of sweetnesse,
48 And lady of lealtee.+

To Love, that lovely is in londe,
I tolde him as I understonde
How this hende hath hent in honde
52 An herte that myn was;
And hir knightes me han so soght—
Sikyng, Sorwyng, and Thoght—
Tho three me han in bale broght
56 Ayeins the power of Pees.

To Love I putte pleyntes mo,
How Sikyng me hath sewed so,
And eke Thoght me thrat to slo+
60 Wyth maistrye if he myghte;
And Sorwe, sore in baleful bend+
That he wolde, for this hende,
Me lede to my lyves ende
64 Unlawefully in lighte.+

44. **bealtee** beauty
46. **pervynke** periwinkle
47. **solsecle** marigold, heliotrope
48. **lealtee** loyalty, faithfulness
59. **thrat to slo** threatened to slay
61. **bend** bondage, bonds
64. **in lighte** openly

45

Love me listned ech a word,
And bowed him to me over bord,
And bad me hente that hord+
68 Of myn herte hele;
"And biseech that swete and swoot,+
Er-than thou falle as fen+ offe foot,
That she wyth thee wol of boot+
72 Dereworthly dele."

For hir love I carke and care,+
For hir love I droupe and dare,+
For hir love my blisse is bare,
76 And al I waxe wan;
For hir love in sleep I slake,
For hir love all nyght I wake,
For hir love murnyng I make,
80 More thanne any man.

65. MS. *Hire* omitted at beginning of line; *ech a* for MS. *vch*.
67. **hord** treasure
69. **swoot** sweet (one)
70. **fen** mud
71. **boot** deliverance, assistance, remedy
73. **carke and care** sorrow and grieve
74. **droupe and dare** languish and lie timidly

46

30

Wynter wakeneth al my care;
Now thise leves waxen bare.
Ofte I sike and murne sare +
4   Whan it cometh in my thoght
    Of this worldes joye, how it goth all to noght.

Now it is and now it nis,
Also it ner nere,+ y-wis.
8 That many man seyth, sooth it is—
    Al goth but Goddes wille;
    Alle we shullen deye, thogh us like ille.

Al that greyn me graveth grene,+
12 Now it faleweth+ al bidene.+
Jhesu, help that it be sene,
    And shilde us from helle;
    For I not+ whider I shal, ne how longe heer dwelle.

Index 4177. MS. Harley 2253. (*RL XIV* No. 9.)
Unique text. *c.* 1320.

3. **sare** = *sore*
7. **ner nere** never had been (*nere* = *ne were*)
11. **that greyn me graveth grene** that grain (seed) that one buries (plants) green (unripe)
12. **faleweth** withers, fades; **bidene** forthwith, quickly
15. **not** = *ne wot* know not

31

Now shrynketh rose and lilye-flour
That whilom bar that swete savour[+]
  In somer, that swete tide;
4 Ne is no quene so stark ne stour,
Ne no lady so bright in bour,
  That deeth ne shal by glyde.
Whoso wol flesshes lust forgon
8   And hevenes blisse abide,
On Jhesu be his thoght anon,[+]
  That thirled was his side.[+]

From Petresburgh in a morwenynge
12 As I me wende on my pleying,
  On my folye[+] I thoghte;
Menen[+] I gan my murnyng
To hire that bar the hevene kyng,
16   Of mercy hire bisoghte:
Lady, preye thy Sone for us
  That us dere boghte,
And shilde us from the lothe hous[+]
20   That to the feend is wroght.

Index 2359. MS. Harley 2253. (*RL XIV* No. 10.)
Unique text. *c.* 1320.

2. **savour** scent
9. **anon** continually, constantly
10. **That thirled was his side** whose side was pierced through
13. **folye** wantonness; foolishness; perhaps illicit love
14. **Menen** complain; communicate, declare in lament
19. **lothe hous** hateful, hideous dwelling-place

Myn herte of dedes was fordred[+]
Of synne that I have my flessh fed
And folwed al my tyme,
24   That I not[+] whider I shal be led
Whan I lie on dethes bed—
   In joye or into pyne.
On a lady myn hope is,
28   Moder and virgine;
We shullen into hevenes blisse
   Thurgh hir medicine.[+]

Bettre is hir medicine
32   Thanne any meed or any wyne;
   Hir herbes smellen swete.
From Catenas into Dyvelyn[+]
Nis ther no leche so fyne
36   Oure sorwes to bete.[+]
Man that feleth any sore[+]
   And his folye wol lete,
Wythouten gold or any tresour
40   He may be sound and sete.[+]

Of penaunce is his plastre[+] al;
And evere serven hire I shal
   Now and al my lyf.
44   Now is free that er was thral,[+]

21. **fordred** terribly frightened
24. **not** = *ne wot* know not
30. **medicine** remedy, cure
34. **From Catenas into Dyvelyn** from Caithness to Dublin
36. **bete** remedy, assuage
37. **sore** pain, grief
40. **sete** content; whole
41. **plastre** (soothing) remedy
44. **thral** enslaved, enthralled

49

Al thurgh that lady gent and smal—
   Heried be hir joyes five!
Wher-so any sik is,
48   Thider hye blive; +
Thurgh hire ben i-broght to blisse
   Bothe mayden and wyf.

For He that dide + his body on tree
52   Of oure synnes have pitee
   That weldeth hevenes boures!
Womman wyth thy jolitee—
Thogh thou be white and bright on blee +—
56   Thou thenk on Goddes shoures. +

. . . .

Falewen + shullen thy floures.
Jhesu, have mercy of us,
60   That al this world honoures. + Amen.

---

48. **hye blive** hasten quickly
51. **dide** placed, put
55. **blee** face, complexion. MS. has line sequence 56, 55, 58, 59, 60; the
    text here follows *RL XIV* No. 10.
56. **shoures** pains, terrors
58. **Falewen** fade, wither
60. **honoures** = *honoreth*

32

Whan the nyghtengale syngeth the wodes waxen grene,
Leef and gras and blosme spryngeth in Aperil, I wene;
And love is to myne herte gon wyth oon spere so kene,
4 Nyght and day my blood it drynketh, myn herte doth me
    tene.+

I have loved al this yeer, that I may love namore;
I have siked many sik, lemman, for thyn ore.
Me nis love nevere the neer, and that me reweth sore:
8 Swete lemman, thenk on me,—I have loved thee yore.

Swete lemman, I preye thee of love oon speche;
While I lyve in world so wide other nyl I seche.
Wyth thy love, my swete leef, my blisse thou myghte
    eche;+
12 A swete cosse of thyn mouth myghte be my leche.

Swete lemman, I preye thee of a love-bene;+
If thou me lovest, as men seyn—lemman, as I wene—
And if it thy wylle be, thou loke that it be sene.
16 So muche I thenke upon thee, that al I waxe grene.

Bitwene Lyncoln and Lindeseye, Northamptoun and
    Lounde,
Ne wot I non so faire a may, as I go forbounde.+
Swete lemman, I preye thee thou love me a stounde;
20 I wol mone+ my song on whom that it is on ylong.+

Index 4037. MS. Harley 2253. (*EL XIII* No. 86.)
Unique text. *c.* 1320.

4. **doth me tene** causes me suffering
11. **eche** increase
13. **I preye thee of a love-bene** to you I pray for a lovers'-boon
18. **forbounde** (MS. *fore ybounde*) bound, enslaved (by love)
20. **mone** mention; **ylong** due

33

As I me rod this endre day
By grene wode to seche pley,+
Wyth herte I thoghte al on a may,
4   Swettest of alle thyng.
Lith+ and I you telle may
    Al of that swete thyng.

This mayden is swete and free of blood,
8 Bright and faire, of mylde mood;
Al she may don us good
    Thurgh hir bisechyng:
Of hire He took flessh and blood,
12   Jhesus, hevenes kyng.

Wyth al my lyf I love that may;
She is my solas nyght and day,
My joye and eke my beste pley,
16   And eke my love-longynge.
Al the bettre me is that day
    That I of hire synge.

Of alle thyng I love hire meste,+
20 My dayes blisse, my nyghtes reste;
She counseileth and helpeth best

Index 359. MS. Harley 2253. (*RL XIV* No. 11.)
Unique text. *c.* 1320.

2. **pley** pleasure
5. **Lith** listen
19. **meste** most, to the greatest extent

Bothe olde and yinge.+
Now I may if that you leste+
24   The five joyes mynge.+

The firste joye of that womman:—
Whan Gabriel from hevene cam
And seyde God sholde bicomen man
28   And of hire be born,
And bryngen up of helle-pyne
    Mankynde that was forlorn.

That othere joye of that may
32   Was on Cristemasse day
Whan God was born on thorugh lay+
    And broghte us lightnesse;+
The sterre was seen bifore day—
36   Thise hierdes+ beren witnesse.

The thridde joye of that lady,
That men clepe the epiphany:—
Whan the kynges comen wery
40   To presente hir sone
Wyth myrre, gold and encense,
    That was man bicome.

22. **yinge** young
23. MS. *nou y may ʒef y wole:* rhyme and meter suggest **If that you leste** If it please you or *If that ye leste* If you will listen; the first emendation has a formulaic quality and relatively light semantic load to recommend it in this context, while the second is recommended by its relation to line 5.
24. **mynge** mention, recall (to mind)
33. **on thorugh lay** in perfect light (?)
34. **lightnesse** light, brightness
36. **hierdes** shepherds

The ferthe joye we telle mowen:
44　On Ester-morwe whan it gan dawen
Hir sone that was slawen
　　Aros in flessh and bon;
More joye ne may me⁺ haven,
48　　Wyf ne mayden non.

The fifte joye of that womman:—
Whan hir body to hevene cam
Hir soule to the body nam⁺
52　　As it was wont to ben.
Crist leve⁺ us alle wyth that womman
That joye al for-to sen.

Preye we alle to oure lady,
56　And to the seintes that wone hire by,
That they of us han mercy,
　　And that we ne mysse⁺
In this world to ben holy
60　　And wynne hevenes blisse.　Amen.

47. **me** one, a person (an indefinite pronoun)
51. **nam** went, took
53. **leve** grant
58. **mysse** miss, fail

54

34

Litel wot it any man
How derne[+] love may stonde,
But it were a free womman
4   That muche of love hadde fonde.[+]
The love of hire ne lasteth nowight[+] longe;
She hath me plight and wyteth me wyth wronge.[+]
Evere and o for my leef I am in grete thoght;
8   I thenke on hire that I ne see not ofte.

I wolde nemne hire to-day
If durste I hire mynne;[+]
She is that fairest may
12 Of ech hende of hir kynne;
But she me love, of me she haveth synne.
Wo is him that loveth the love that he ne may ner y-wynne.
Evere and o for my leef I am in grete thoght;
16 I thenke on hire that I ne see not ofte.

Adoun I fil to hire anon
And cried, "Lady, thyn ore!
Lady, have mercy of thy man—
20 Leve[+] thou no fals lore!

Index 1921. MS. Harley 2253. (*EL XIII* No. 91.)
Unique text. *c.* 1320.

2. **derne** secret, not divulged; profound, intense (?)
4. **fonde** had experience with, made trial of
5. **nowight** not a bit, not at all
6. **wyteth me wyth wronge** blames me wrongfully
10. **If durste I hire mynne** If I dared call her to mind; MS. *ant y dorste hire munne*
18. **cried** for MS. *crie*
20. **leve** believe

If thou dost it wol me rewe sore.
Love dreccheth[+] me that I ne may lyve namore."
Evere and o for my leef I am in grete thoght;
24 I thenke on hire that I ne see not ofte.

Myrie it is in hir tour
Wyth hatheles[+] and wyth hewes;[+]
So it is in hir bour
28 Wyth gamenes and wyth glewes.
But she me love, sore it wol me rewe.
Wo is him that loveth the love that ner nyl be trewe.
Evere and o for my leef I am in grete thoght;
32 I thenke on hire that I ne see not ofte.

Fairest fode[+] upon-lofte,[+]
My gode leef, I thee grete
As fele sithe[+] and ofte
36 As dewes dropes ben wete,
As sterres ben in welkne[+] and grases soure and swete.
Whoso loveth untrewe,[+] his herte is selde sete.[+]
Evere and o for my leef I am in grete thoght;
40 I thenke on hire that I ne see not ofte.

22. dreccheth afflicts
26. hatheles men, heroes; hewes servants
33. fode creature; upon-lofte alive
35. fele sithe many times, repeatedly
37. welkne sky
38. untrewe (one who is) untrue; sete content, satisfied

56

35

Litel wot it any man
How love Him hath i-bounde
That for us on the rode ran
4   And boghte us wyth His wounde.
The love of Him us hath i-maked sounde,+
And i-cast the grimly gost+ to grounde.
Evere and o, nyght and day, He hath us in His thoght;
8   He nyl not lese that+ He so dere boghte.

He boghte us wyth His holy blood—
What sholde He don us more?
He is so meke, mylde, and good,
12   He nagulte+ not ther-fore.
That+ we han y-don I rede we rewen sore,
And crien evere to Jhesu, "Crist, thyn ore."
Evere and o, nyght and day, He hath us in His thoght;
16   He nyl not lese that He so dere boghte.

He saw His Fader so wonder wroth+
Wyth man that was i-falle,
Wyth herte sore He seyde his oth
20   We sholde a-beyen+ alle.
His swete sone to Him gan clepe and calle,

Index 1922. MS. Harley 2253. (*EL XIII* No. 90.)
Unique test (but see *EL XIII*, pp. 235–237). C. 1320.

5. **sounde** healed, having salvation
6. **grimly gost** terrible (-looking) spirit, i.e., the Devil
8. **that** i.e., that which
12. **nagulte** (= *ne agulte*) did not sin
13. **that** i.e., (for) that which
17. **wonder wroth** wondrously angry
20. **a-beyen** pay the penalty for; redeem

And preyde He moot deyen for us alle.
Evere and o, nyght and day, He hath us in His thoght;
24 He nyl lot lese that He so dere boghte.

He broghte us alle from the deeth
And dide us frendes dede.
Swete Jhesu of Nazareth,
28 Thou do us hevenes mede:
Upon the rode why nol+ we taken hede?
His grene+ wounde so grimly gonne+ blede.
Evere and o, nyght and day, He hath us in His thoght;
32 He nyl not lese that He so dere boghte.

His depe woundes bleden faste;
Of hem we oghte mynne.+
He hath us out of helle i-cast,
36 I-broght us out of synne.
For love of us His wonges+ waxen thynne;
His herte blood He yaf for al mankynne.
Evere and o, nyght and day, He hath us in His thoght;
40 He nyl not lese that He so dere boghte.

29. **nol** = *ne wol* will not
30. **grene** fresh, freshly made (*EL XIII* reads *greue*, *HL* reads *grene*);
   gonne did
34. **mynne** remember, hold in mind
37. **wonges** cheeks

36

Al nyght by the rose, rose—
  Al nyght by the rose I lay;
  Durste I noght the rose stele,
4 And yet I bar the flour awey.

Index 194. MS. Rawlinson D. 913. (*SL XIV-XV* No. 17.)
Unique text. After 1300.

37

I am of Irelond,
And of the holy lond
Of Irelond.

Gode sire, preye I thee,
For-of + Seint Charitee
Come and daunce wyth me
4   In Irelond.

Index 1008. MS. Rawlinson D. 913. (*SL XIV-XV* No. 15.)
Unique text. After 1300.

2. **For-of** for the sake of

38

Mayden in the moor lay—
In the moor lay—
  Seven-nyght fulle,
4   Seven-nyght fulle.
Mayden in the moor lay—
In the moor lay—
  Seven-nyghtes fulle and a day.

8 Wel+ was hir mete.
What was hir mete?
  The prymerole+ and the—
    The prymerole and the—
12 Wel was hir mete.
What was hir mete?
  The prymerole and the vyolete.

Wel was hir drynke.
16 What was hir drynke?
  The colde water of the—
    The colde water of the—
Wel was hir drynke.
20 What was hir drynke?
  The colde water of the welle-spryng.

Index 3891. MS. Rawlinson D. 913. (*SL XIV-XV* No. 18.)
Unique text. After 1300.

8. **Wel** good
10. **prymerole** primrose

Wel was hir bour.
What was hir bour?
24 The rede rose and the—
  The rede rose and the—
Wel was hir bour.
What was hir bour?
28 The rede rose and the lilye-flour.

39

Lullay, lullay, litel child, why wepest thou so sore?
Nedes most thou wepe, it was i-yarked[+] thee yore—
Evere to lyve in sorwe, and sike and murne evere,
As thyne eldres dide er this, whil they alyve were.
    Lullay, lullay, litel child, child lullay, lullow,
    Into uncouth world i-comen so art thou.

Bestes and tho foules, the fisshes in the flood,
And ech shaft[+] alyve i-maked of bon and blood—
Whan they comen to the world they don hem-selve som
    good,
Alle but the wrecche brolle[+] that is of Adames blood.
    Lullay, lullay, litel child, to care art thou bimette;[+]
    Thou nost[+] noght this worldes weild,[+] bifore thee is i-set.

Child, if bitide that thou shalt thrive and thee,[+]
Thenk thou wast i-fostred upon thy modres knee;
Evere have mynde in thyn herte of tho thynges three—
Whan[+] thou comest, whan thou art, and what shal come of
    thee.
    Lullay, lullay, litel child, child lullay, lullay,
    Wyth sorwe thou cam into this world, wyth sorwe shalt
        wende awey.

Index 2025. MS. Harley 913. (*RL XIV* No. 28.)
Unique text. *c.* 1320.

Ne trust thou to this world, it is thy ful fo—
20 The riche it maketh poure, the poure riche also;
It turneth wo to wele and eke wele to wo—
Ne trust no man to this world whil it turneth so.
    Lullay, lullay, litel child, the foot is in the wheel;
24   Thou nost whider turne to wo other wele.

Child, thou art a pilgrim in wikkednesse i-bore;
Thou wandrest in this false world—thou loke thee bifore.
Deeth shal come wyth a blast oute of a wel dim hore⁺
28 Adames kyn doun to kaste, him-self hath i-don bifore.
    Lullay, lullay, litel child, so wo thee warp⁺ Adam
    In the lond of paradys thurgh wikkednesse of Satan.

Child, thou nart⁺ a pilgrim but an uncouth gest;
32 Thy dayes ben i-told, thy journeys⁺ ben i-cast.
Whider thou shalt wende, north other est,
Deeth thee shal bitide wyth bitter bale in brest.
    Lullay, lullay, litel child, this wo Adam thee wroght
36   Whan he of the appel eet, and Eve it him bitaughte.⁺

20. *it* for MS. *he*
27. **wel dim hore** very dark mist, quite obscuring fog. See *OED* **haar**
29. **warp** wove, prepared
31. **nart** = *ne art*
32. **journeys** days
36. **bitaughte** gave

40

The lady Fortune is bothe freend and fo:
Of poure she maketh riche, of riche poure also;
She turneth wo al into wele, and wele al into wo.
4 Ne truste no man to this wele, the wheel it turneth so.

41

Hond by hond we shullen us take,
And joye and blisse shullen we make,
For the devel of helle man hath forsake,
And Goddes Sone is maked oure make.

A child is born amonges man,
And in that child was no wam; +
That child is God, that child is man
4 And in that child oure lyf bigan.

Synful man, be blithe and glad,
For youre mariage thy pees is grad +
   Whan Crist was born!
8 Com to Crist—thy pees is grad;
For thee was his blood i-shad,
   That were forlorn.

Synful man, be blithe and bold,
12 For hevene is bothe boght and sold
   Everich a foot!
Com to Crist—thy pees is told;
For thee he yaf a hundredfold
16   His lyf to boot. +

Index 29. MS. Bodley 26. (*RL XIV* No. 88.)
One other partial text. *c.* 1350.

2. **wam** blemish, stain
6. **pees is grad** peace is proclaimed
16. **to boot** as compensation, salvation

42

Lullay, lullay, litel child, child rest thee a throwe,[+]
From heighe hider art thou sent wyth us to wonen lowe;
Poure and litel art thou made, uncouth and unknowe,
4 Pyne and wo to suffren heer for thyng that nas[+] thyn owe.
    Lullay, lullay, litel child, sorwe myghte thou make;
    Thou art sent into this world, as thou were forsake.

Lullay, lullay, litel grome,[+] kyng of all thyng,
8 Whan I thenke of thy myschief me listeth wel litel synge;
But caren I may for sorwe, if love were in myn herte,
For swiche peynes as thou shalt dreyen[+] were nevere non
    so smerte.
    Lullay, lullay, litel child, wel myghte thou crie,
12 For-than thy body is bleik and blak,[+] soon after shal ben
    drye.

Child, it is a wepyng dale that thou art comen in;
Thy poure cloutes[+] it proven wel, thy bed made in the
    bynne;
Cold and hunger thou most tholen, as thou were geten[+] in
    synne,
16 And after deyen on the tree for love of alle mankynne.

Index 2023. Advocates Lib. 18. 7. 21. (*RL XIV* No. 65.)
Unique text. *c.* 1370.

1. **a throwe** for a time
4. **nas** = *ne was,* replacing MS. *was*
7. **grome** boy
10. **dreyen** suffer, endure
12. **bleik and blak** pallid and pale
14. **cloutes** clouts; (fragments of) cloth worn as clothing
15. **geten** begotten

Lullay, lullay, litel child, no wonder thogh thou care,
Thou art comen amonges hem that thy deeth shullen
    yare.+

Lullay, lullay, litel child, for sorwe myghte thou grete;+
20 The anguissh that thou suffren shalt shal don the blood to
    swete;
Naked, bounden shaltow ben, and sithen sore bete,
No thyng free upon thy body of pyne shal ben lete.+
    Lullay, lullay, litel child, it is al for thy fo,
24   The harde bond of love-longyng that thee hath bounden
    so.

Lullay, lullay, litel child, litel child, thyn ore!
It is al for oure owene gilt that thou art peyned sore.
But wolden we yet kynde ben and lyven after thy lore,
28 And leten synne for thy love, ne keptest thou no more.+
    Lullay, lullay, litel child, softe sleep and faste,
    In sorwe endeth every love but thyn atte laste.

18. **yare** prepare, bring about
19. **grete** weep, cry
22. **lete** left, omitted
28. **ne keptest thou no more** you would not receive the blows (of punishment) any more (for us), i.e., your suffering (in atonement for our
sins) would be at an end. *keptest* is preterit subjunctive; see *OED* **kep**
and **keep** (verb).

43

Whan men beth muriest at her mele
Wyth mete and drynke to maken hem glade,
Wyth worshipe and wyth worldly wele,
4 They ben so sete⁺ they conne not sade.⁺
They han no deyntee⁺ for-to dele
Wyth thynges that ben devoutly made;
They wene her honour and her hele
8 Shal evere laste and nevere diffade.⁺
But in her hertes I wolde they hadde,
Whan they gon richest men on array,
How soon that God hem may degrade,
12 And som tyme thenken on yesterday.

This day, as leef we mowen ben lighte,
Wyth alle the myrthes that men mowen vise⁺
To revel wyth thise burdes brighte,
16 Ech man gayest on his gise.⁺
Atte laste it draweth to nyght,
That sleep moot maken his maistrise;⁺
Whan that he hath i-kid⁺ his myght,
20 The morwe he busketh⁺ up to rise,—
Than al draweth him to fantasyse:
Wher he is bicomen can no man seye—

Index 3996. Vernon MS. (*RL XIV* No. 101.)
One other text. *c.* 1370.

4. **sete** content; **sade** become serious, be concerned
5. **deyntee** fondness, pleasure
8. **diffade** fade, pass away
14. **vise** devise
16. **gise** style, fashion
18. **maistrise** mastery, domination
19. **i-kid** made known, manifested
20. **busketh** makes ready, prepares

And if they wiste they weren ful wyse—
24 For al is turned to yesterday.

Whoso wolde thenke upon this
Myghte fynde a good enchesoun⁺ why
To preve⁺ this world, alwey, y-wis.
28 It nis but fantom and fairye:⁺
This erthly joye, this worldly blisse,
Is but a fikel fantasye,
For now it is and now it nis—
32 Ther may no man ther-inne affye;⁺
It chaungeth so ofte and so sodeynly,—
To-day is heer, to-morwe awey.
A siker ground⁺ he wole him gye⁺
36 I rede he thenke on yesterday.

For ther nis non so strong in stour,⁺
From tyme that he ful waxen be,
From that day forth everich an houre
40 Of his strengthe he leest⁺ a quantitee.
Ne no burde so bright in bour
Of thritty wynter, I ensure thee,
That she ne shal faden as a flour—
44 Lite and lite⁺ lesen her beautee.
The sooth ye mowen your-selven ysee
Ben youre eldres, in good fey;
Whan ye ben grettest in youre degree
48 I rede ye thenken on yesterday.

26. **enchesoun** reason, cause
27. **preve** test
28. **fairye** illusion, magical contrivance
32. **affye** trust
35. **A siker ground** (if) on sure ground, on a certain foundation; **gye**
(reflexive verb) conduct himself
37. **stour** battle
40. **leest** loses
44. **lite and lite** little by little

Nis non so fressh on foot to fare,+
Ne non so faire on folde+ to fynde,
That they ne shullen on bere+ be broght ful bare.
52   This wrecched world nis but a wynd,
Ne non so stif+ to stynte ne stare,
Ne non so bold beres to bynde
That he nath+ warnynges to be war.
56   For God is so curteis and so kynde,
Bihold the lame, the bedrede, the blynde,
That bidde you be war while that ye may: +
They maken a mirour to youre mynde
60   To see the shap of yesterday.

The lyf that any man shal lede
Beth certeyn dayes atte laste;
Than moste oure terme shorte nedes,+
64   Be oon day comen another is passed.
Heer-of if we wolden take good hede
And in oure hertes acountes caste,
Day by day, wythouten drede,
68   Toward oure ende we drawen ful faste;
Than shullen oure bodies in erthe be thrast,+
Oure careynes+ couched under cley.
Heer-of we oghte ben sore agast,
72   If we wolden thenke on yesterday.

---

49. **non . . . on foot to fare** no one to go on foot, i.e., anyone at all
50. **fold** earth
51. **bere** bier
53. **stif** strong, valiant
55. **nath** = *ne hath*
58. **may** = *mowen*
63. **moste oure terme shorte nedes** must our term (time of life) necessarily shorten
65. *if* for MS. *and* here and in l. 72
69. **thrast** thrust, put
70. **careynes** dead bodies

Salomon seyde, in his poesye,
He holdeth wel bettre wyth an hound
That is likyng and joly,
76 And of siknesse hol and sound,
Thanne be a leoun+ thogh he lie
Cold and deed upon the grounde.
Wher-of serveth his victorie,
80 That was so stif in ech a stounde?
The moste fool, I herde respounde,+
Is wyser whil he lyven may,
Thanne he that hadde a thousand pound
84 And was buried yesterday.

Socrates seyth a word ful wys:
It were wel bettre for-to see
A man that now parteth+ and deyes+
88 Thanne a feste of realtee.+
The feste wol maken his flessh to rise,
And drawe his herte to vanytee;
The body that on the bere lies+
92 Sheweth the same that we shullen be.
That fereful fit+ may no man flee,
Ne wyth no wyles wynne it awey:
Ther-fore among al jolitee
96 Som tyme thenk on yesterday.

But yet me merveileth over al
That God lett many man croke+ and elde,
Whan myght and strengthe is from hem falle,

77. **leoun** lion
81. **respounde** answer
87. **parteth** departs; **deyes** = *deyeth*
88. **feste of realtee** sumptuous, splendid feast
91. **lies** = *lieth*
93. **fit** terrible or violent experience
98. **croke** become bent, crooked

71

100 That they mowen not hem-selven a-welde; +
And now thise beggars most principal
That good ne profit mowen non yelde.
To this purpose answere I shal
104 Why God sente swiche men boot and belde: +
Crist that made bothe flour and feeld
Lett swiche men lyven, for-sothe to seye,
Whan a yong man on hem biheld
108 Sholde see the shap of yesterday.

Another skile + ther is for-why
That God lett swiche men lyven so longe:
For they ben treacle + and remedye
112 For synfulle men that han don wronge.
In hem the sevene dedes of mercy
A man may fulfille among,
And also thise proude men mowen ther-by
116 A faire mirour underfonge. +
For ther nis non so stif ne strong,
Ne no lady so stout ne gay,—
Bihold what over her hed can honge,
120 And som tyme thenk on yesterday.

I have wist, sith I coude mynne, +
That children han by candel light
Her shadwe on the wal i-seen
124 And ronne ther-after al the nyght.
Bisy aboute they han ben
To cacchen it wyth al her myght;

100. **a-welde** control, maintain rule
104. **boot and belde** relief and comfort
109. **skile** reason, argument
111. **treacle** salve, remedy
116. **underfonge** take
118. *so* not in MS.
121. **mynne** remember

And whan they cacchen it best wolden wene,
128 Sannest+ it schet+ out of her sight.
The shadwe cacchen they ne myghte,
For no lynes+ that they coude leye.
This shadwe I may likne aright
132 To this world and yesterday.

Into this world whan we ben broght
We shullen be tempt to covetise,+
And al thy wit shal be thurgh-soght
136 To more good thanne thou mowe suffise.
Whan thou thenkest best in thy thoght
On richesse for-to regne and rise,
Al thy travaile turneth to noght,
140 For sodeynly on deeth thou deyes.+
Thy lyf thou hast i-lad wyth lyes,+
So this world gan thee bitraye:
Ther-fore I rede thou this despise
144 And som tyme thenke on yesterday.

Man, if thy neighebore thee manace,+
Other+ to kille or to bete,
I knowe me siker in the cas+
148 That thou wolt drede thy neighebores threte,
And nevere a day thy dore to passe
Wythouten siker defence and grete,
And ben purveied in ech a place
152 Of sikernesse and help to gete.

128. **Sannest** suddenly, quickly; **schet** vanishes
130. **lynes** lines, cords (for catching birds)
134. **covetise** covetousness, avarice
140. **deyes** = *deyest*
141. **lyes** falsehood
145. **manace** menace, threaten
146. **other** either
147. **siker in the cas** assuredly in that circumstance

73

Thyn enemy woltow not forgete
But ay be aferd of his affray.
Ensaumple⁺ heer-of I wol thee trete⁺
156 To maken thee thenke of yesterday.

Wel thou wost wythouten faile
That deeth hath manaced thee to deye,
But whan that he wol thee assaile,
160 That wost thou not, ne nevere most spye.
If thou wolt don by my counseil,
Wyth siker defence be ay redy;
For siker defence in this bataile
164 Is clene lyf, parfit, and trie.⁺
Put thy trust in Goddes mercy,
It is the best at al assay,
And evere among thou thee en-nuye⁺
168 Into this world and yesterday.

Som men seyn that deeth is a theef
And al unwarned wol on hem stele;
And I seye nay, and make a preef⁺
172 That deeth is stedefast, trewe, and lele,⁺
And warneth ech man of his greef
That he wol oon day wyth him dele.
That lyf that is to you so leef
176 He wol you reve, and eke youre hele—
Thise poyntes may no man him repele;
He cometh so boldely to pike⁺ his pray,
Whan men beth muriest at her mele,—
180 I rede ye thenken on yesterday.

---

155. **ensaumple** instance; **trete** discuss, set forth. Here and in line 156
thee replaces MS. *3ou.*
164. **trie** excellent
167. **en-nuye** become weary (reflexive verb)
171. **preef** proof
172. **lele** loyal, faithful
178. **pike** get, pick out, plunder

74

44

My cares comen evere anewe—
   A! dere God, no boot ther nis,
For I am holden for untrewe
4   Wythouten gilt, so have I blisse.

To be trewe woned⁺ I was
   In any thyng that I myghte don;
I thonked God his grete grace:
8   Now it is I may noght don.

Index 2231. MS. Douce 381. (*SL XIV-XV* No. 150.)
With music. Unique text. *c.* 1390.

5. **woned** accustomed

45

"A! Sone, tak hede to me whos sone thou wast
And set me wyth thee upon thy cros—
Me heer to leve and thee hennes thus go:
4   It is to me greet care and endeles wo.
Stynt now, sone, to be hard to thy moder,
Thou that were evere goodly to al othere."

"Stynt now, Moder, and weep namore;
8   Thy sorwe and thy disese greve me ful sore.
Thou knowest that in thee I took mannes kynde,
In this for mannes synne to be thus pyned.
Beth now glad, Moder, and have in thy thoght
12   That mannes hele⁺ is founde that I have soght.
Thou shalt not now care⁺ what thou shalt don,
Lo! John thy cosyn shal be thy sone."

Index 14. Balliol Coll. Oxf. MS. 149. (*RL XIV* No. 128.)
One other text. *c.* 1390.

12. **hele** salvation
13. **care** have concern, solicitude

46

Marie moder, wel thee be!
Marie mayden, thenk on me!
Moder and mayden was nevere non
4 Togidre, lady, but thou allone.

Marie moder, mayden clene,
Shilde me from sorwe and tene;[+]
Marie, out of synne help thou me,
8 And out of dette for charitee.

Marie, for thy joyes five,
Help me to lyve in clene lyve;
For the teres thou lette under the rode,
12 Send me grace of lyves fode[+]

Wher-wyth I may me clothe and fede,
And in trouthe my lyf lede.
Help me, lady, and alle myne,
16 And shilde us alle from helle-pyne.

Shilde me, lady, from vilanye,[+]
And from alle wikked companye;
Shilde me, lady, from wikked shame,
20 And from alle wikked fame.

Index 2119. MS. Rawlinson liturgical g.2. (*RL XIV* No. 122.)
Forty-eight other texts extant. Before 1400.

6. **tene** suffering, affliction, grief
12. **fode** sustenance, livelihood
17. **vilanye** shameful, ignominious conduct; villainy

Swete lady, thou me were[+]
That the feend noght me dere;[+]
Bothe by day and by nyght
24 Help me, lady, wyth thy right.

For my frendes I bidde thee
That they mowen amended be,
Bothe to soule and to lyf,
28 Marie, for thy joyes five.

For my fo-men I bidde also
That they mowen heer so do
That they in wraththe heighe ne deye,
32 Swete lady, I thee preye.

They that ben in gode lyve,
Marie, for thy joyes five,
Swete lady, ther-inne hem holde,
36 Bothe the yonge and the olde.

And that[+] ben in deedly synne,
Ne lat hem nevere deye ther-inne;
Marie, for thy joyes alle,
40 Lat hem nevere in helle falle.

Swete lady, thou hem rede
That they amenden of her mysdede;
Biseech thy Sone, hevenes kyng,
44 That He me graunte good endyng;

And sende me, as He wel may,
Shrift and housel at myn endyng-day;
And that we mowen thider wende
48 Ther joye is wythouten ende. Amen. Amen.

21. **were** protect, ward off (affliction), guard
22. **dere** afflict, injure
37. **that** i.e., those who

47

Wyth a gerlond of thornes kene
Myn hed was crouned, and that was sene;
The stremes of blood ronne by my cheke: SUPERBIA[+]
4   Thou proude man, lerne to be meke.

Whan thou art wroth and woldest take wreche,[+]
Kepe wel the lore that I thee teche;
Thurgh my right hond the nayle goth: IRA
8   Foryeve ther-fore and be not wroth.

Wyth a spere sharp and gril[+]
Myn herte was wounded, wyth my wyl,
For love of man that was me dere: INUIDIA
12   Envious man, of love thou lere.

Ris up, Lust,[+] out of thy bed,
Thenk on my feet that are for-bledde
And harde nayled upon a tree: ACCIDIA
16   Thenk on, man, this was for thee.

Index 4185. Camb. Univ. Lib. Ff. 5. 48. (Henry A. Person, *Cambridge Middle English Lyrics*, Revised edition, 1962, No. 8.)
One other text. *c.* 1400.

   Superbia Pride, one of the Seven Deadly Sins. The others, listed beside
   the stanzas, are **Ira** Wrath, **Inuida** Envy, **Accidia** Sloth, **Auaricia**
   Avarice, **Gula** Gluttony, and **Luxuria** Lechery. **Ihesuc** Jesus
   5. **wreche** vengeance
   9. **gril** harsh, cruel
13. **Lust** pleasure. The other text (in *RL XIV* No. 127) reads *vnlust*
   sluggard.

Thurgh my left hond the nayle was dryven—
Thenk ther-on, if thou wylle lyven;
And worship God wyth almes-dede,   AUARICIA
20   That at thy deyng hevene may be thy mede.

In alle my peynes I suffred on rode
Man yaf me drynke no thyng gode—
Eisel⁺ and galle for-to drynke: GULA
24   Glotoun, ther-on evere thou thenk.

Of a mayden I was born
To save the folk that weren forlorn;
Al my body was beten for synne: LUXURIA
28   Lechour, ther-fore I rede thee blynne.

I was beten for thy sake—
Synne thou leve and shrift thou tak;
Forsak thy synne and love me,   IHESUC
32   Amend thee, and I foryeve thee.

17. *left* for MS. *right*
23. **Eisel** vinegar

48

Esto memor mortis iam porta sit omnibus ortis
  Sepe sibi iuuenes accipit ante senes.+

Sith al that in this world hath ben *in rerum natura,*
  Or in this wide world was seen *in humana cura,*
  Alle shullen passe wythouten ween+ *via mortis dura;*
4 God graunte that mannes soule ben clene *penas non passura.*
  Whan thou leeste wenest,+ *veniet mors te superare:*
  Thus thy grave greveth,+ *ergo mortis memorare.*

Vnde vir extolleris, thou shalt be wormes mete,
8 *Qui quamdiu vixeris* thy synnes woldest thou not lete;
  Quamuis diues fueris and of power greet,
  Cum morte percuteris help myghte thou non gete.
  Si diues fias do thy-self good, man, wyth thyne hondes;
12   *Post necis ergo uias* ful fewe wol lose+ thee of thy bondes.

Index 3122. Camb. Univ. MS. Ee. 6. 29. (*RL XIV* No. 135.)
Four other texts. *c.* 1400.

Be mindful of death: now there is a gate for all men born; often it
takes to itself young men before old. (Hereafter, all Latin passages are
glossed without notice within the text of the poem.)
1. in the nature of things, i.e., in the created world
2. in human care
3. **ween** doubt. along the hard way of death
4. (so as) not to suffer punishment
5. **leeste wenest** least expect. death will come to overwhelm you
6. **greveth** afflicts with sorrow; or (?) inters, swallows up. therefore
   remember death.
7. when you, as a man, will be carried away, or, when, O man, you are
   (to be) carried away.
8. who as long as you will live
9. although you will have been rich
10. when you will be shattered by death
11. if you would be rich
12. after the ways of death. **lose** loosen, free

This oghte wel to felle+ thy pride, *quod es moriturus;*
Thou knowest neither tyme ne tide *qua es decessurus.*
Wormes shullen ete thy bak and side, *inde sis securus:*
16 As thou hast wroght in this world wide *sic es recepturus.*
   Thus deeth thee ledeth, *terre tumilo quasi nudum;*
   Deeth no man dredeth, *mors terminat hiccine ludum.*

Nam nulli vult parcere deeth that is un-dere,+
20 *Pro argenti munere,* ne for non faire preyere;
Sed dum rapit propere, he chaungeth ech mannes chere,+
In peccati scelere if he be founden heer.
   Set cum dampnatis helle to thy mede thou wynnest,
24 That nevere blynneth *pro peccatis sceleratis.*

Whan I thenke upon my deeth, *tunc sum contristatus,*
And waxe as hevy as any leed+ *meos ob reatus;*
Deeth turneth into wrecchedhede+ *viros magni status,*
28 Than may no thyng stonde in stede *mundi dominatus.*
   Wyth ful bare bones *mundi rebus cariturus,*
   Thus from thise wones+ *transit numquam rediturus.*

13. **felle** destroy, put down. the fact that you are going to die
14. at which you are going to descend
15. of that you may be sure
16. so you are going to receive
17. in a mound of earth as if naked
18. death ends the game at this point
19. for he is willing to spare no one. **un-dere** hated, feared
20. for a gift of money
21. while he snatches you quickly away. **chere** appearance
22. in (an evil) deed of sin
23. but with the damned
24. for thy wicked sins
25. then I am sorrowful
26. **leed** lead. on account of my thoughts
27. **wrecchedhede** (state of) wretchedness. men of high standing
28. the lordship (rule) of the world
29. to lack (be absent from) the world
30. **wones** dwellings, abodes. you pass never to return

Caro vermis ferculum, thenk on the pynes of helle;
32 *Mors habet spiculum* that smyteth man ful felle; +
Te ponet ad tumilum til domes-day to dwelle.
Hic relinquis seculum; ther nis noght elles to telle.
    Mors cito cuncta rapit; ther-fore, man, thenk on thy
        werkes.
36   Thus seyn thise clerkes: *mors cito cuncta rapit.*

God that deyde on the tree *pro nostra salute,*
And aros after dayes three *diuina uirtute,*
Yif us grace synne to flee *stante iuuentute,*
40 On domes-day that we mowen see *vultum tuum tute.*
    Dolful deeth drede I thee, *veniet quia nescio quando:*
    Be redy ther-fore, I warne thee, *de te peccata fugando.*

---

31. flesh is a worm's dish
32. death has a dart (arrow). **felle** cruelly, destructively
33. he will place you in the tomb
34. you leave, here, the world (behind)
35. death carries all things quickly off
36. death carries all things quickly off
37. for our salvation
38. by divine power
39. while youth lasts
40. thy countenance safely
41. because he will come I know not when
42. by putting thy sins to flight from thee

49

In a tabernacle⁺ of a tour,
As I stood musyng on the mone,
A crouned quene, most of honour,
4   Appered in gostly sight ful soon.
She made compleynte thus by hir oon
For mannes soule was wrapped in wo:
"I may not leve mankynde allone
8   *Quia amore langueo.*⁺

"I longe for love of man my brother;
I am his vocate⁺ to voide⁺ his vice,
I am his moder—I can non other.
12   Why sholde I my dere child despise?
If he me wrathe⁺ in diverse wyse,
Thurgh flesshes freeltee⁺ falle me fro,
Yet mote we rewe him til he rise,
16   *Quia amore langueo.*

"I bidde, I bide in greet longynge;
I love, I loke whan man wol crave;
I pleyne for pitee of peynynge.
20   Wolde he axe mercy he sholde it have.
Sey to me, soule, and I shal save;
Bid me, my child, and I shal go;
Thou preydest me nevere but my Sone foryaf,—
24   *Quia amore langueo.*

Index 1460. MS. Douce 322. (*RL XIV* No. 132.)
Eight other texts of varying extent. *c.* 1400.

1. **tabernacle** = (?) niche (in a wall), covered seat
8. **Quia amore langueo** because I languish (swoon) with love
10. **vocate** advocate, intercessor; **voide** expel, remove
13. **If he me wrathe** If he should provoke me to anger
14. **freeltee** frailty. *Thurgh* for MS. *Though*
15. *me* (from other MSS.) replacing *we*

84

"O wrecche in the world, I loke on thee;
I see thy trespas day by day
Wyth lechery ayeins my chastitee,
28 Wyth pride ayeins my poure array.
My love abideth, thyn is awey;
My love thee calleth, thou stelest me fro;
Sewe+ to me synner, I thee preye,
32   *Quia amore langueo.*

"Moder of mercy I was for thee made.
Who nedeth it but thou allone?
To gete thee grace I am more gladde
36 Thanne thou to axe it—why woltow non?
Whan seyde I nay, tel me, to oon?
For sothe, nevere yet to freend ne fo.
Whan thou axest noght, than make I mone,
40   *Quia amore langueo.*

"I seche thee in wele and wrecchednesse,
I seche thee in richesse and povertee.
Thou man, bihold wher thy moder is!
44 Why lovest thou me not sith I love thee?
Synful or sory, how evere thou be,
So welcome to me ther are no mo.
I am thy suster; right trust on me,—
48   *Quia amore langueo.*

"My child is outlawed for thy synne,
My child is beten for thy trespas;
Yet priketh myn herte that so nigh my kyn
52 Sholde be disesed. —O Sone, allas!

---

31. **Sewe** (from another MS.) petition, replacing MS. *shewe*
50. *My child is beten for thy trespas* from another MS., replacing *Man-kynde ys bette for hys trespasse*

Thou art his brother! Thy moder I was—
Thou soukedest my pappe! Thou lovedest man so,
Thou deydest for him! Myn herte he has,
56   *Quia amore langueo.—*

"Man, leve thy synne than for my sake!
Why sholde I yeve thee that thou not wolde? +
And yet if thou synne, som preyere tak
60 Or trust in me as I have tolde.
Am not I thy moder called?
Why sholdest thou flee? I love thee, lo!
I am thy freend, thy help, bihold!
64   *Quia amore langueo.—*

"Now, Sone," she seyde, "woltow seye nay
Whan man wolde mende him of his mys? +
Thou lette me nevere in vayne yet preye.—
68 Than, synful man, see thou to this,
What day thou comest, welcome thou is
This hundreth yeer, if thou were me fro;
I take thee ful fayne, I clyppe, I kisse,
72   *Quia amore langueo.*

"Now wol I sitte and seye namore,
Leve and loke + wyth greet longynge;
Whan a man wol calle I wol restore.
76 I love to save him, he is myn ofsprynge;

---

53. *Thy* (from another MS.) replacing *hys*
58. **wolde** = *woldest*
62. *Why sholdest thou flee* (from other MSS.) replacing *Why shulde I flee the*
63. *thy help* (from another MS.) replacing *I helpe*
66. **mys** wrongdoing, offenses
74. **Leve and loke** cease and wait (expectantly)

86

No wonder if myn herte on him hynge.+
He was my neighebore—what may I do?
For him hadde I this worshipynge,
80   And therefore *quia amore langueo*.

"Why was I crouned and made a quene?
Why was I called of mercy the welle?
Why sholde an erthly womman ben
84   So heighe in hevene above aungel?
For thee, mankynde, the trouthe I telle!
Thou axe me help and I shal do
That+ I was ordeyned—kepe thee from helle,
88   *Quia amore langueo*.

"Now, man, have mynde on me for evere;
Loke on thy love thus languisshyng;
Lete us nevere from other dissevere.+
92   Myn help is thyn owene, creep under my wyng;
Thy suster is a quene, thy brother is a kyng;
This heritage is tailed,+ soon com ther-to!
Tak me for thy wyf and lerne to synge,
96   *Quia amore langueo*."

77. **hynge** hang
87. **that** i.e., that which
91. **dissevere** separate
94. **tailed** entailed
95. *wyf.* Another MS. reads *moder*

50

In the vale of resteles mynde
I soghte in mountayne and in meed
Trustyng a trewe-love for-to fynde.
4 Upon an hil than took I hede;
A vois I herde (and neer I yede[+])
In greet dolour compleynyng tho:
"See, dere soule, my sides blede,
8 *Quia amore langueo.*"[+]

Upon this mount I fond a tree;
Under this tree a man sittyng.
From hed to foot wounded was he,
12 His herte blood I saw bledyng;
A seemly man to ben a kyng,
A gracious face to loke unto.
I axed him how he hadde peynyng:
16 He seyde, "*Quia amore langueo.*

"I am trewe-love that fals was nevere;
My suster, mannes soule, I lovede hire thus:
Bicause I wolde on no wyse dissevere[+]
20 I lefte my kyngdom glorious;

Index 1463. Camb. Univ. Lib. Hh. 4.12, with variants from Lambeth MS. 853. (Both in F. J. Furnivall, ed., *Political, Religious, and Love Poems*, EETS OS. 15 [1866].)
Two texts. *c.* 1430.

5. **yede** went, walked
8. **Quia amore langueo** because I languish (swoon) with love
19. **dissevere** separate

I purveiede+ hire a place ful precious.
She flitte, I folwed, I lovede hire so
That I suffred thise peynes piteous,
24 *Quia amore langueo.*

"My faire love and my spouse brighte
I savede hire from betyng and she hath me bette;
I clothede hire in grace and hevenly light:
28 This blody sherte+ she hath on me set.
For longyng love I wol not lete.+
Swete strokes ben thise, lo!
I have loved evere as I hette,+
32 *Quia amore langueo.*

"I crounede hire wyth blisse and she me wyth thorn;
I ledde hire to chambre and she me to deye;
I broghte hire to worshipe and she me to scorn:
36 I dide hire reverence and she me vilanye.+
To love that+ loveth is no maistrye;
Hir hate made nevere my love hir fo.
Axe than no more questiouns why,
40 But *quia amore langueo.*

"Loke unto myne hondes, man!
Thise gloves were yeven me whan I hire soghte.
They ben not white, but rede and wan;+
44 Enbrouded wyth blood my spouse hem boghte.

---

21. **purveiede** provided
28. **sherte** shirt, from Lambeth MS., replacing *surcote*
29. **lete** cease
31. **hette** promised; *evere* replaces MS. *ouer*
36. **vilanye** shameful, ignominious conduct, villainy
37. **that** i.e., that one who
43. **wan** dark

They wol not offe; I leve hem noght;
I wowe hire wyth hem wher-evere she go.
Thise hondes ful freendly for hire foghte,
48   *Quia amore langueo.*

"Merveil not, man, thogh I sitte stille,—
My love hath shod me wonder streyte: +
She bokeled my feet, as was hir wylle,
52   Wyth sharpe nayles—wel thou mayst waite. +
In my love was nevere disceite,
For alle my membres I have opened hire to;
My body I made hir hertes baite, +
56   *Quia amore langueo.*

"In my side I have made hir neste.
Loke in, how wide a wounde is heer:
This is hir chambre, heer shal she reste,
60   That she and I mowen slepe in fere. +
Heer may she wasshe if any filthe were;
Heer is socour for al hir wo.
Come if she wyl, she shal have chere,
64   *Quia amore langueo.*

"I wol abide til she be redy;
I wol to hire sende er she seye nay;
If she be reccheles + I wol be redy,
68   If she be daungerous + I wol hire preye;

50. **wonder streyte** very closely, tightly
52. **waite** look, observe
55. **baite** lure, enticement
58. *Loke in,* omitting *me,* as in Lambeth MS.
60. **in fere** together, as companions
67. **reccheles** without care, negligent
68. **daungerous** disdainful

If she do wepe than bidde I nay:
Myne armes ben sprad to clyppe⁺ hire to.
Cry ones⁺ 'I come,' now, soule, assay,
72   *Quia amore langueo.*

"I sitte on an hil for to see fer;
I loke to the vale my spouse to see.
Now renneth she aweyward, now cometh she nere,
76   Yet from myn eye-sight she may not be.
Som wayte her pray to make hire flee,
I renne to-fore to fleme⁺ hir fo.
Retourn, my soule, ageyn to me,
80   *Quia amore langueo.*

"My swete spouse, lat us go pleye—
Apples ben ripe in my gardyn;
I shal thee clothe in newe array,
84   Thy mete shal be milk, hony, and wyne.
Now, dere soule, lete us go dyne—
Thy sustenaunce is in my scrippe,⁺ lo!
Tary not now, faire spouse myn,
88   *Quia amore langueo.*

---

70. **clyppe** clasp
71. **ones** once
74. *to see,* from Lambeth MS., replacing *I see*
78. **fleme** put to flight, from Lambeth MS., replacing *chastise*
79. *Retourn,* from Lambeth MS., replacing *recouer*
81. *lat us,* from Lambeth MS., replacing *will we*
83. *thee clothe,* from Lambeth MS., replacing *clothe the*
86. **scrippe** bag, wallet (for food)

"If thou be foule I shal make thee clene;
If thou be sik I shal thee hele;
If thou aught murne I shal thee mene.+
92 Spouse, why wyltow not wyth me dele?
Thou founde nevere love so lele.+
What wyltow, soule, that I shal do?
I may of unkyndenesse thee appele,+
96   *Quia amore langueo.*

"What shal I do now wyth my spouse?
Abide I wol hir gentilnesse.
Wolde she loke ones out of hir hous
100 Of flesshly+ affecciouns and unclennesse,
Hir bed is made, hir bolster is in blisse,
Hir chambre is chosen, swiche are no mo.
Loke out at the wyndowes of kyndenesse,
104   *Quia amore langueo.*

"My spouse is in chambre—hold thy pees!
Make no noise, but lat hire slepe.
My babe shal suffre no disese;
108 I may not here my dere child wepe;
For wyth my pappe I shal hire kepe.
No wonder thogh I tende hire to,
This hole in my side hadde nevere ben so depe,
112   But *quia amore langueo.*

89. *thee* not in MS.
91. **mene** pity. *thee mene*, from Lambeth MS., replacing *be-mene*
93. **lele** loyal, faithful
95. **appele** accuse
100. **flesshly** worldly; carnal-minded
105-120. Here the order of the two stanzas is reversed, following **Lambeth MS.**

"Longe and love thou nevere so heighe,
Yet is my love more thanne thyn may be;
Thou gladdest, thou wepest, I sitte thee by;
116 Yet myghte thou, spouse, loke ones at me.
Spouse, sholde I alwey fede thee
Wyth childes mete? Nay, love, not so!
I wol preve⁺ thy love wyth adversitee,
120   *Quia amore langueo.*

"Wax not wery, myn owene dere wyf!
What mede is ay to lyve in confort?
For in tribulacioun I regne more rife
124 Ofter tymes thanne in desport;⁺
In welthe, in wo, evere I supporte.
Than, dere soule, go nevere me fro—
Thy mede is marked, whan thou art mort⁺
    In blisse; *quia amore langueo.*"

---

119. **preve** test. *I wol preve thy love,* from Lambeth MS., replacing *I pray the love*
124. **desport** amusement, entertainment
127. **mort** dead

51

Deo gracias anglia,
Redde pro victoria.

Oure kyng went forth to Normandy
Wyth grace and myght of chivalry;
Ther God for him wroghte merveilously,
4   Wherfor Englond may calle and crie:
     "*Deo gracias!*"

He sette a sege,⁺ the soth for-to seye,
To Harflu toun⁺ wyth royal array;⁺
8   That toun he wan and made affray⁺
   That Fraunce shal rewe til domesday.
     Deo gracias!

Than went oure kyng wyth al his ost⁺
12   Thurgh Fraunce, for al the Frenshe bost;⁺
   He spared no drede⁺ of leest ne most
   Til he cam to Agincourt cost.⁺
     Deo gracias!

Index 2716. MS. Arch. Selden B. 26. (*HP XIV-XV* No. 32.)
One other version. "The Agincourt Carol," on the occasion of
  Henry V's famous victory at Agincourt; perhaps used in cele-
  brations upon Henry's return to London. With music. 1415.

   Deo . . . victoria Return thanks to God, England, for victory
  6. **He sette a sege** he lay siege
  7. **To Harflu toun** before Harfleur; **array** display of military force
  8. **affray** disturbance, terror (caused by attack or fighting)
 11. **ost** (military) host, army
 12. **bost** boast, vaunt, threatening
 13. **He spared no drede** he shunned no dreaded things, he did not keep
    clear of (things of) danger
 14. **cost** district, bordering area

16 Than for sothe that knight comly
In Agincourt feeld he faught manly;
Thurgh grace of God moste myghty
He hadde bothe the feeld and the victorie.
20 *Deo gracias!*

Ther dukes and erles, lord and baroun,
Were take and slayn, and that wel soon;
And som were led in-to Londoun
24 Wyth joye and myrthe and greet renoun.+
Deo gracias!

Now gracious God he save oure kyng,
His peple, and alle his wel-wyllyng;+
28 Yeve him good lyf and good endyng,
That we wyth myrthe mowe saufly synge:
"*Deo gracias!*"

24. **renoun** display, distinction
27. **wel-wyllyng** well-wishers, i.e., friends

52

Querela diuina

O Man unkynde, have in mynde
   My peynes smerte!
Bihold and see that is for thee
4   Perced myn herte.

And yet I wolde, er-than[+] thou sholde
   Thy soule forsake,
On cros wyth peyne sharp deeth ageyn
8   For thy love take.

For which I axe non other taske
   But love ageyn.
Me than to love alle thynges above
12   Thou oghte ben fayn.

Responsio humana

O Lord, right dere, thy wordes I here
   Wyth herte ful sore;
Ther-fore from synne I hope to blynne
16   And greve[+] no more.

Index 2504. B.M. Addit. MS. 37049. (*RL XV* No. 108.)
Two other texts, one of which is a copy of an inscription in
  Almondbury Church, Yorkshire. *c.* 1430.

5. **er-than** before, sooner; rather than
16. **greve** cause pain (to)

But in this cas now helpe thy grace
    My freelnesse, +
That I may evere don thy plesure
20   Wyth lastyngnesse.

This grace to gete, thy modres eke,
    Evere be proon, +
That we mowen alle into thy halle
24   Wyth joye come soon. Amen.

18. **freelnesse** frailness, frailty
22. **proon** eager, prone, ready (in mind)

53

Adam lay i-bounde,
   Bounden in a bond;
Foure thousand wynter
4   Thoghte he not to longe.
And al was for an appel,
   An appel that he took,
As clerkes fynden writen
8   In here book.

Ne hadde the appel take ben,
   The appel take ben,
Ne hadde nevere oure lady
12   A ben hevenes quene.
Blessed be the tyme
   That appel take was,—
Ther-fore we mowen synge
16   *"Deo gracias."*

Index 117. MS. Sloane 2593. (*RL XV* No. 83.)
Unique text. *c.* 1430.

54

I synge of a mayden
That is makeles:
Kyng of alle kynges
4   To hir sone she ches.⁺

He cam also stille⁺
Ther⁺ his moder was
As dewe in Aprill
8   That falleth on the gras.

He cam also stille
To his modres bour
As dewe in Aprill
12   That falleth on the flour.

He cam also stille
Ther his moder lay
As dewe in Aprill
16   That falleth on the spray.

Moder and mayden
Was nevere non but she:
Wel may swich a lady
20   Goddes moder be.

Index 1367. MS. Sloane 2593. (*RL XV* No. 81.)
Unique text. *c.* 1430.

4. **ches** chose
5. **also stille** as silently, as gently
6. **Ther** (there) where

55

Now bithenk thee, gentilman,
How Adam dalf and Eve span.+

In the vale of Abraham
Crist him-self he made Adam,
And of his ryb a faire womman;
4   And thus this seemly world bigan.

"Com, Adam, and thou shalt see
The blisse of paradys that is so free;
Ther-inne stant an appel-tree—
8   Leef and fruyt growen ther-on.

"Adam, if thou this appel ete,
Alle thise joyes thou shalt foryete+
And the peynes of helle gete."
12   Thus God him-self warned Adam.

Whan God was from Adam gon,
Soon after cam the feend anon—
A fals traitour he was oon.
16   He took the tree and crepte ther-on.

"What eyleth thee, Adam, art thou wood?
Thy Lord hath taught thee litel good!
He wolde not thou understood
20   Of the wyttes+ that he can.

Index 1568. MS. Sloane 2593. (*EEC* No. 336.)
Unique text. *c.* 1430.

> **Adam dalf and Eve span** Adam labored (by digging) and Eve spun.
> This is a formula put to several uses over several generations; cf. *OED*
> **delve.**
> 10. **foryete** lose, give up
> 20. **wyttes** (things of) knowledge, wisdom

"Tak the appel offe the tree
And ete ther-of, I bidde thee,
And alle thise joyes thou shalt see;
24   From thee he shal hiden non."

Whan Adam hadde that appel ete,
Alle thise joyes weren foryete;
Non word more myghte he speke.
28   He stood as naked as a ston.

Than cam an aungel wyth a swerd
And drof Adam into a desert;
Ther was Adam sore aferd,
32   For labour coude he werke non.

56

I have a yong suster
  Fer biyonde the see;
Many ben the drueries[+]
4   That she sente me.

She sente me the chery
  Wythouten any ston,
And so she dide the dowve
8   Wythouten any bon.

She sente me the brere[+]
  Wythouten any rynde,[+]
She bad me love my lemman
12   Wythouten longynge.

How sholde any chery
  Ben wythouten ston?
And how sholde any dowve
16   Ben wythouten bon?

How sholde any brere
  Ben wythouten rynde?
How sholde I love my lemman
20   Wythouten longynge?

Index 1303. MS. Sloane 2593. (*SL XIV-XV* No. 45.)
Unique text, but similar paradoxes are common. *c.* 1430.

3. **drueries** presents, keepsakes; (?) love tokens
9. **brere** (stock of) a wild rose
10. **rynde** bark (of a plant)
19. *sholde I love* for MS. *xuld love.*

Whan the chery was a flour,
Than hadde it non ston;
Whan the dowve was an ey,[+]
24   Than hadde it non bon.

Whan the brere was unbred,[+]
Than hadde it non rynde;
Whan the mayden hath that she loveth,
28   She is wythouten longynge.

23. **ey** egg
25. **unbred** unborn, i.e., a seed

57

How! hey! It is non lees,+
I dar not seyn+ whan she seyth "Pees!"

Yonge men, I warne you everichoon,
Elde wyves taketh ye non—
For I my-self have oon at hom:
4   I dar not seyn whan she seyth "Pees!"

Whan I come from the plough at noon,
In a riven dissh my mete is don;
I dar not axen oure dame a spoon—
8   I dar not seyn whan she seyth "Pees!"

If I axe oure dame breed,
She taketh a staf and breketh myn hed,
And doth me rennen under the bed.
12   I dar not seyn whan she seyth "Pees!"

If I axe oure dame flessh,
She breketh myn hed with a dissh:
"Boy,+ thou art not worth a rissh!"
16   I dar not seyn whan she seyth "Pees!"

If I axe oure dame chese,
"Boy," she seyth, al at ese,
"Thou are not worth half a pese!"+
20   I dar not seyn whan she seyth "Pees!"

Index 4279. MS. Sloane 2593. (*SL XIV-XV* No. 43.)
Unique text. *c.* 1430.

    lees lie, falsehood
    seyn say (anything), i.e., speak
15. **Boy** worthless fellow (used contemptuously in addressing a person)
19. **pese** pea, hence "you are worthless" (cf. line 15)

58

Synge we alle and seye we thus:
Gramercy,+ myn owene purs.

Whan I have in my purs ynough,
I may have bothe hors and plough
And also frendes ynough—
4   Thurgh the vertu of my purs.

Whan my purs gynneth to slake,
And ther is noght in my pak,
They wol seyn, "Go! Farewel, Jakke,
8   Thou shalt namore drynke wyth us."

Thus is al my good i-lorn,
And my purs is al to-torn;+
I may pleye wyth an horn
12   In the stede al of my purs.

Farewel, hors, and farewel, cow,
Farewel, carte, and farewel, plough;
As I pleyde me wyth a bowe
16   I seyde, "God, what is al this?"

Index 72. MS. Sloane 2593. (*EEC* No. 385.)
Unique text. *c.* 1430.

Gramercy literally, great thanks; thank you
10. **to-torn** torn to pieces. *is* not in MS.

59

God be wyth Trouthe wher he be;
I wolde he were in this contree!

A man that sholde of Trouthe telle,
Wyth grete lordes he may not dwelle;
In trewe storie, as clerkes telle,
4   Trouthe is put in lowe degree.

In ladies chambres cometh he not,
Ther dar Trouthe sette non foot;
Thogh he wolde he may not
8   Come among the heighe meynee.⁺

Wyth men of lawe he hath non space,
They loven Trouthe in non place;
Me thinketh they han a rewely⁺ grace
12   That Trouthe is put at swich degree.

In Holy Chirche he may not sitte,
From man to man they shullen him flitte;⁺
It reweth me sore in my wyt—
16   Of Trouthe I have greet pitee.

Index 72. MS. Sloane 2593. (*EEC* No. 385.)
Unique text. *c.* 1430.

8. **heighe meynee** fine company
11. **rewely** rueful, pitiable
14. **flitte** shift, pass on

Religious,[+] that sholden be gode,
If Trouthe come ther, I holde him wood;
They sholden him rende cote and hood
20   And maken him bare for-to flee.

A man that sholde of Trouthe espye,
He moot sechen esily[+]
In the bosom of Mary,
24   For ther he is for sothe.

17. **Religious** those in religious orders
22. **esily** calmly, quietly

60

I passed thurgh a gardyn grene,
I fond an herber made ful newe;
A seemlier sight I have not seen—
4   On ilke tree song a turtel trewe.
Ther-inne a mayden bright of hewe,
And evere she song and nevere she cessed;
Thise were the notes that she gan shewe:
8   *"Verbum caro factum est."*⁺

I axed that mayden what she mente,
She bad me bide and I sholde here;
What she seyde I took good tente—
12   In hir song hadde she vois ful clere.
She seyde, "A prince wythouten pere
Is born and leyd bitwene two beste;⁺
Ther-fore I synge as thou mayst here,
16   '*Verbum caro factum est.*'"

And thurghout that frith⁺ as I gan wende,
A blisful song yet herde I mo;
And that was of three shepherdes hende:
20   *"Gloria in excelsis deo."*
I wolde not they hadde faren me fro,
And after hem ful faste I prest;
Than tolde they me that they songen so,
24   For *verbum caro factum est.*

Index 378. Advocates MS. 19. 3. 1. (*RL XV* No. 78.)
Another version in MS. Sloane 2593. *c.* 1430.

  8. **Verbum caro factum est** the word is made flesh
14. **beste** = *bestes* beasts
17. **frith** woodland, forest
18. *song* supplied from Sloane MS.

They seyde that song was this to seye:
"To God above be joye and blisse,
For pees in erthe also we preye
28 To alle men that in goodnesse is.
The may that is wythouten mys+
Hath born a child bitwene two beste;
She is the cause ther-of, y-wis,
32 That *verbum caro factum est.*

I fared me furthe+ in that frith,
I mette three comly kynges wyth croune;
I spedde me forth to speke hem wyth,
36 And on my knees I knelede doun.
The royalest of hem to me gan roune+
And seyde, "We fared wel at the feste;
From Bethleem now are we boun,+
40 For *verbum caro factum est.*

"For we sawen God bicomen in mannes flessh,
That boot+ has boght of al oure bale,
Awey oure synnes for-to wasshe;
44 A may him herberd in hir halle,
She socoured him soothly in hir sall+
And held that hende in hir arest;+
Ful trewely may she telle that tale
48 That *verbum caro factum est.*"

29. **mys** fault
33. **furthe** onward
37. **roune** address
39. **boun** preparing to go
42. **boot** redress, salvation
45. **sall** hall, chamber
46. **arest** abiding-place, chamber

Unto that princesse wol we preye,
As she is bothe moder and mayde;
She be oure help as she wel may
52 To him that in hir lappe was leyd;
To serve him we ben prest and payed,⁺
And ther-to make we oure biheste;
For I herde when she song and seyde,
56 *"Verbum caro factum est."*

53. **prest and payed** ready and content

61

Go, litel bille, and do me recomaunde
Unto my lady wyth goodly countenaunce;
For trusty messager I thee sende.
4 Preye hire that she make purveiaunce,+
For my love, thurgh hir suffraunce,+
In hir bosom desireth to reste,
Sith of alle wommen I love hire beste.

8 She is lilye of redolence
Which only may don me plesure;
She is the rose of confidence
Most confortyng to my nature.
12 Unto that lady I me assure,
I wyl hire love and nevere mo:—
Go, litel bille, and sey hire so.

She resteth in my remembraunce
16 Day other nyght wher-so I be;
It is my special daliaunce+
For-to remembre hir beautee.
She is enprented in ech degree
20 Wyth yiftes of nature inexplicable,
And eke of grace incomparable.

Index 927. MS. Douce 326. (*RL XV* No. 46.)
Unique text. Fifteenth century.

4. **purveiaunce** provision
5. **suffraunce** permission, allowance
15. *resteth* replaces MS. *restyd*
17. **daliaunce** delight

The cause ther-fore, if she wyl wite,
Why I presume on swich a flour?
24 Sey of hire (for it is i-write)
She is the fairest paramour,
And to man in ech langour
Most soverayn mediatrice: +
28 Ther-fore I love that flour of pris.

Hir beautee hoolly to descrive,
Who is he that may suffise?
For sothe no clerk that is alyve,
32 Sith she is only wythouten vice.
Her flavour excedeth the flour-de-lys;
Aforn alle floures I have hire chose
Entierly in myn herte to close.

36 Hire I biseche (sith I not feyne,
But only putte me in hir grace)
That of me she not desdeyne,
Takyng regard at old trespas,—
40 Sith myn entente in every place
Shal be to don hir obeisaunce +
And hire to love sauns variaunce.

23. *Why* replaces MS. *Wyll*
27. **mediatrice** mediator, intercessor
30. *he* replaces MS. *she*
41. **obeisaunce** (act of) submission, homage, obeisance

62

How come alle ye that ben i-broght
In bondes, ful of bitter bisynesse
Of erthly lust abidyng in youre thoght?
4 Heer is the reste of al youre bisynesse:
Heer is the port of pees, and restfulnesse
To hem that stonde in stormes of disese,
Only refuge to wrecches in distresse,
8 And al comfort of myschief and mysese.

Index 1254. Royal MS. 9. C. ii. (*RL XV* No. 164.)
Unique text. Fifteenth century.

63

I moot go walke the wode so wilde,
    And wandren heer and ther
    In drede and deedly fere;
4 For wher I trusted I am bigiled,
    And al for oon.

Thus am I banysshed from my blisse
    By craft and fals pretence,
8   Fautles wythoute offence;
As of retourn no certeyn⁺ is,
    And al for fere of oon.

My bed shal be under the grene-wode tree,
12   A toft of brakes⁺ under myn hed,
    As oon from joye were fled;
Thus from my lyf day by day I flee,
    And al for oon.

16 The rennyng stremes shullen be my drynke,
    Accornes shullen be my fode;
    No-thyng may do me good
But whan of thy beautee I do thenke—
20   And al for love of oon.

Index 1333. Huntington MS. EL 1160. (*SL XIV-XV* No. 20.)
Unique text. Fifteenth century.

9. **certeyn** certainty
12. **toft of brakes** tuft of ferns or bracken

64

Go, litel ryng, to that ilke swete
  That hath myn herte in hir demeyne,+
And loke thou knele doun at hir feet
4   Bisechyng hire she wolde not desdeyne
  On hir smale fyngres thee to streyne;+
    Than I wyl thee seye boldely:
    "My maister wolde that he were I."

Index 932. Royal MS. 17. D. vi. (*SL XIV-XV* No. 95.)
Unique text. Fifteenth century.

2. **demeyne** possession, demesne
5. **streyne** encircle, clasp

65

Fressh lusty beautee joyned wyth gentilesse,
  Demure, apert, + glad chere wyth governaunce, +
Ech thyng demened by avysenesse, +
4   Prudent of speche, wysdom of daliaunce, +
Gentilesse wyth wommanly plesaunce,
  Hevenly eyen, aungelik of visage—
  Al this hath nature set in thyn ymage.

8   Wythe trouthe wyth Penelope, +
And wyth Grisilde parfit pacience,
Like Polixene fairely on-to see,
  Of bountee + beautee having the excellence
12   Of Quene Alceste, and al the diligence
  Of faire Dido, princesse of Cartage—
  Al this hath nature set in thyn ymage.

Index 869. Trinity Coll. Camb. MS. 600. (*SL XIV-XV* No. 131.)
By John Lydgate (?1370-1449). One other text.

2. **Demure, apert** reserved, frank, open; **governaunce** government, self-control
3. **avysenesse** deliberation
4. **daliaunce** conversation
8. **Penelope** Odysseus' wife ingeniously withstood suitors who thought her husband was dead. See Homer's *Odyssey*. (Other proper names are glossed without notice in text.)
9. **Grisilde** In legend, her perfect patience in suffering outrageous cruelty is ultimately rewarded. See Chaucer's *Clerk's Tale*.
10. **Polixene** Daughter of Priam, king of Troy, she was sacrificed at the end of the Trojan War.
11. **bountee** excellence, virtue
12. **Alceste** The only one willing to die in place of her husband Admetus, Alcestis was rescued by Heracles.
13. **Dido** Having fallen in love with Aeneas, Dido killed herself when he left her. Cf. Chaucer's *Legend of Good Women*.

Of Niobe the seur perseveraunce,
16   Of Adriane the grete stedefastnesse,
Assured trouthe, void of variaunce;
    Wyth yong Tesbee ensaumple of kyndenesse,
    Of Cleopatres abidyng stablenesse,
20   Mekenesse of Hester void of al outrage⁺—
    Al this hath nature set in thyn ymage.

Beautee surmountyng wyth faire Rosemounde,
    And wyth Isoude for-to ben secree,⁺
24 And like Judith in vertue to habounde,
    And seemlynesse wyth Quene Bersabee,
    Innocence, freedom, and heighe bountee,
    Fulfilled of vertue void of al damage—
28   Al this hath nature set in thyne ymage.

15. **Niobe** Punished for pride by the gods, the grieving Niobe was turned to stone.
16. **Adriane** Ariadne was abandoned on an island by her husband Theseus. Cf. Chaucer's *Legend of Good Women*.
18. **Tesbee** Thisbe, lover of Pyramus. Cf. Chaucer's *Legend of Good Women*.
19. **Cleopatra** Cf. Chaucer's *Legend of Good Women* and Plutarch's account of Antony in *Lives of the Noble Grecians and Romans*.
20. **Hester** Esther. See the Book of Esther. **outrage** intemperance
22. **Rosemounde** Rosamond "The Fair," mistress of Henry II of England.
23. **Isoude** Isolt (Iseult), in the Tristan legends. **secree** trusty, secret
24. **Judith** Slayer of Holofernes. See the apocryphal Book of Judith.
25. **Bersabee** Bathsheba. See II Samuel.

What sholde I more reherce of wommanhede?
   Thou best the mirour and verray exemplaire+
Of whom that word and thoght accorde in dede;
32   And in my sight fairest of alle faire,
      Humble and meke, benigne and debonaire,
         Of othere vertues wyth al the surplusage+
         Which that nature hath set in thyn ymage.

36   I see non lak but only that Daunger
      Hath in thee voided Mercy and Pitee,
   That thee list not wyth thyn excellence
      Upon thy servauntes goodly for-to see;
40   Wher-on ful sore I compleyne me
         That Routhe+ is void to my disavauntage,
         Sith alle thise vertues ben set in thyn ymage.

                  L'envoye
         Go, litel balade, and recomaund me
44   Unto hir pitee, hir mercy, and hir grace—
   But firste be war aforn that thou wel see+
      Desdayn and Daunger ben void out of that place;
      For elles thou mayst have leiser non nor space+
48   Trewely to hire to don my message,
         Which hath alle vertues set in hir ymage.

30. **exemplaire** perfect specimen
34. **surplusage** surplus, abundance
41. **Routhe** Pity, Compassion
45. **see** = *seest*
47. **leiser . . . space** opportunity . . . occasion

66

So faire, so fressh, so goodly on-to see,
   So wel demened in al thy governaunce[+]
   That to myn herte it is a greet plesaunce
4 Of thy goodnesse whan I remembre me;
   And truste fully wher that evere I be
   I wyl abide under thy obeisaunce,—[+]
So faire, so fressh, so goodly on-to see,
8   So wel demened in al thy governaunce.
For in my thoght ther is no mo but thee
   Whom I have served wythoute repentaunce:
   Wher-fore, I preye thee, sethe[+] to my grevaunce,
12 And put aside al myn adversitee,—
So faire, so fressh, so goodly on-to see,
   So wel demened in al thy governaunce.

Index 3162. Paris Bibl. nat. MS. f. fr. 25458. (*SL XIV-XV* No. 182.)

By Charles d'Orleans (1391-1455). One other text.

2. **governaunce** government, self-control, demeanor
6. **obeisaunce** obedience, (act of) attention, homage
11. **sethe** look (to), (= *see thou?*)

67

Go forth, myn herte, wyth my lady;
  Loke that thou spare no bisynesse+
  To serve hire wyth swich lowlynesse
4 That thou gete hir grace and mercy;
Preye hire ofte-tymes prively
  That she kepe trewely hir promesse:
Go forth, myn herte, wyth my lady,
8   Loke that thou spare no bisynesse.
I moot as a herteles body
  Abide allone in hevynesse,+
  And thou shalt do wel wyth thy maistresse
12 In plesaunce glad and myrie,—
Go forth, myn herte, wyth my lady,
  Loke that thou spare no bisynesse.

Index 922. Paris Bibl. nat. f. fr. 25458. (*SL XIV-XV* No. 183.)
By Charles d'Orleans (1391-1455). Two other texts.

2. **bisynesse** diligence, careful attention
10. **hevynesse** dejection, sorrow

68

Go herte, hurt wyth adversitee,
   And lat my lady thy woundes see;
And sey hire this, as I seye thee:
4   Farewel my joye, and welcome peyne,
   Til I see my lady ageyn.

Index 925. MS. Ashmole 191. (*SL XIV-XV* No. 155.)
With music (a madrigal). Unique text. *c.* 1445.

69

Allas, departyng is ground of wo,—
   Other song can I not synge.
But why parte I my lady fro,
4   Sith love was cause of oure metyng?
   The bittre teres of hir wepyng
      Myn herte hath perced so mortally,
   That to the deeth it wil me brynge
8   But if I see hire hastily.

Index 146. MS. Ashmole 191. (*SL XIV-XV* No. 156.)
With music. Unique text. *c.* 1445.

70

Now wolde I fayn som myrthes make
Al only for my ladies sake,
   Whan I hire see;
4 But now I am so fer fro hire
   It wol not be.

Thogh I be fer out of hir sight,
I am hir man bothe day and nyght,
8   And so wol be:
Ther-fore wolde as I love hire
   She lovede me.

Whan she is myrie than am I glad,
12 Whan she is sory than am I sad,
    And cause is why:—
For he lyveth not that loveth hire
   So wel as I.

16 She seyth that she hath seen it writen
That 'selden seen is soon forgeten.'
    It is not so,
For, in good feith, save only hire
20   I love no mo.

Wher-fore I preye bothe nyght and day
That she may caste al care awey
    And lyve in reste,
24 And evermore wher-evere she be
    To love me best;

Index 2381. MS. Ashmole 191. (*SL XIV-XV* No. 171.)
Another text in Camb. Univ. MS. Ff. 1. 6. *c.* 1445.

And I to hire to be so trewe,
And nevere to chaunge for no newe,
28   Unto myn ende,
And that I may in hir servise
    Evere to amende.

71

My gostly fader, I me confesse,
    First to God and than to you,+
    That at a wyndow (wost thou how?)
4   I stal a cosse of greet sweetnesse,
    Which don was out avysenesse;+
    But it is don, not undon, now,
My gostly fader, I me confesse,
8   First to God and than to you.
But I restore it shal douteles
    Ageyn, if so be that I mowe,—+
    And that to God I make avow,
12 And elles I axe foryifnesse.
    My gostly fader, I me confesse
    First to God and than to you.

Index 2243. Harley MS. 682. (*SL XIV-XV* No. 185.)
Unique text. *c.* 1450.

2. **you** = *thee*
5. **avysenesse** deliberation
10. **mowe** for *mote* (subjunctive), or *may*
11. **MS.** reads: *And that god y make a vow*

72

As in thee resteth my joye and confort,
Thy disese is my mortal peyne;
Soon God sende me swich report
4   That may conforte myn herte in every veyne.
Who but thou may me susteyne,
Or of my greef be the remedye,
But thou soon have amendement of thy maladye?

8 Which is to me the hevyest remembraunce
That evere can be thoght in any creature;
Myn herte hangyng thus in balaunce
Til I have knoweleche and verraily sure
12   That God in thee hath list don this cure,
Of thy disese to have allegeaunce⁺
And to be releved of al thy grevaunce.

Index 383. Camb. Univ. MS. Ff. 1. 6. (*SL XIV-XV* No. 164.)
Unique text. Before 1500.

13. **allegeaunce** alleviation, relief

73

Allas, allas the while!
Thoghte I on no gile,
So have I good chaunce.
Allas, allas the while—
That evere I coude daunce!

Ledde I the daunce a mydsomer day;
I made smal trippes,⁺ soth for-to seye.
Jak, oure holy water clerk, cam by the weye,
4 And he loked me upon, he thoghte that I was gay.
    Thoghte I on no gile.

Jak, oure holy water clerk, the yonge strippelyng,⁺
For the chesoun of me⁺ he cam to the ryng;
8 And he tripped on my too⁺ and made a twynkelyng⁺—
Evere he cam neer, he spared for no thyng.
    Thoghte I on no gile.

Jak, I wot, pryed⁺ in my faire face;
12 He thoghte me worly,⁺ so have I good grace.
As we turnden oure daunce in a narwe place,
Jak bad me the mouth—a kissing ther was.
    Thoghte I on no gile.

Index 1849. Caius Coll. Camb. MS. 383. (*SL XIV-XV* No. 28.)
Unique text. Expansions and emendations as in *SL XIV-XV*
    No. 28. *c.* 1450.

2. **trippes** steps in dancing
6. **strippelyng** a youth just passed into manhood, stripling
7. **For the chesoun of me** because of me
8. **too** toe; **twynkelyng** wink
11. **pryed** looked searchingly
12. **worly** attractive

¹⁶ Jak tho bigan to roune in myn ere,⁺
"Loke that thou be privee and graunte that thou bere;
A paire white gloves I have to thy were."⁺
"Gramercy, Jak," that was myn answere.
²⁰   Thoghte I on no gile.

Soon after evensong Jak me mette:
"Com hom after thy gloves that I thee bihete."
Whan I to his chambre cam, doun he me sette;
²⁴ From him myghte I not go whan we were mette.
     Thoghte I on no gile.

Shetes and chalones,⁺ I wot, were i-spred;
For sothe tho Jak and I wenten to bed.
²⁸ He priked and he praunced—nolde⁺ he nevere lynne:⁺
It was the muriest nyght that evere I cam inne.
     Thoghte I on no gile.

Whan Jak hadde don tho he rong the belle;
³² Al nyght ther he made me to dwelle.
Oft, I trewe,⁺ we hadden i-served the ragged⁺ devil of helle;
Of other smal bourdes⁺ kepe I not to telle.
     Thoghte I on no gile.

16. **roune in myn ere** whisper in my ear
18. **were** i.e., wearing
26. **Shetes and chalones** sheets and blankets
28. **nolde** = *ne wolde;* **lynne** cease
33. **trewe** suppose; **ragged** shaggy
34. **bourdes** frivolities, delights

36 The other day at pryme+ I cam hom, as I wene,
    Mete I my dame copped and kene:+
    "Sey, thou stronge strompet, wher hastow+ ben?
    Thy trippyng and thy daunsyng, wel it wol be sene!"
40   Thoghte I on no gile.

    Evere by oon and by oon+ my dame raughte me clout.+
    Evere I bar it privee whil that I moghte,+
    Til my girdel aros, my womb wex out:
44 "Yvele i-spun yerne+ evere it wol out."
        Thoghte I on no gile.

36. **The other day at pryme** the next morning at dawn (before sunup)
37. **copped and kene** peevish, bad-tempered and harsh
38. **hastow** = *hast thou*
41. **Evere by oon and by oon** again and again; **raughte me clout** dealt me a clout, a cuff (with the hand)
42. **moghte** = *myghte*
44. **Yvele i-spun yerne** ill-spun yarn

74

Care awey, awey, awey,
Murnyng awey,
 I am forsake,
 Another is take,
No more murne I may.

I am sory for hir sake,
 I may wel ete and drynke;
Whan I slepe I may not wake,
4 So muche on hire I thenke.

I am broght in swich a bale,
 And broght in swich a pyne,
Whan I rise up of my bed
8 Me liste wel to dyne.

I am broght in swich a pyne
 I-broght in swich a bale,
Whan I have riche gode wyne
12 Me liste drynke non ale.

Index 1280. Caius Coll. Camb. MS. 383. (*SL XIV-XV* No. 37.)
Unique text. *c.* 1450.

75

I may wel sike for grevous is my peyne
Now to departe from thee this sodeynly;
My faire swete herte, thou causest me to compleyne;
4 For lak of thee I stonde ful pitously
Al in disconfort, wythouten remedye.
Most in my mynde, my lady soverayne,
Allas, for wo! departyng hath me slayn.

8 Farewel, my myrthe, and chief of my confort;
My joye is turned into hevynesse
Til I ageyn to thee may resorte;
As for the tyme I am but recureles, +
12 Like to a figure which that is herteles.
Wyth thee it is, God wot, I may not feyne,
Allas, for wo! departyng hath me slayn.

Yet not wythstondyng, for al my grevaunce,
16 It shal be taken right paciently,
And thenk it is to me but a plesaunce
For thee to suffre a greet deel more trewely;
Wyl nevere chaunge but kepe unfeynyngly
20 Wyth al my myght to be bothe trewe and playn:
Allas, for wo! departyng hath me slayn.

Index 1331. Camb. Univ. MS. Ff. 1. 6. (*SL XIV-XV* No. 169.)
Unique text. *c.* 1470.

11. **recureles** lacking (in means or hope) of recovery

76

Faire, fresshest erthly creature
   That evere the sonne over-shon,
The best and the shapliest figure
4   That kynde hath wroght of blood and bon—

. . . .

   Whos I have ben, am, and evere shal be in oon:
    Wyth al my poure hertes lowe servise
8   I me recomaunde on every humble wyse
    That tonge can telle or herte devise,
To thee that alle my lyves are on.

My trouthe to thee I write
12   As he that is wyth wo oppressed sore,
Compleynyng, as I dar endite,
   My hele that is evermore.
Al-thogh thise wordes rude ben and lite,
16   Be thou not greved wyth me there-fore.
    Biseche I thy noble grace,
    And hold not thy debonaire face
    Defouled to see this whan thou hast space,
20   That boot[+] is of my sorwe sore.

Index 754. MS. Douce 95. (*SL XIV-XV* No. 199.)
(Among the difficulties in this text are the apparent omission of
   a line after line 5 and the corruption of line 36.) Unique text.
   Fifteenth century.

16. *Be thou*, replacing MS. *ye be*
19. *thou hast*, replacing MS. *I have*, probably for *ye have*
20. **boot** cure

Thy goodnesse also I biseche
   Consider al myn hertes care;
Thou lette thy mercy over me strecche,
24   And that causeth my mysfare
(As this lettre shal thee shewe),
   My lyves ende, my blisse bare.
    Thou vouchesauf to me to dele
28   Right as thee list, siknesse or hele,
    Lyf or deeth, wo or wele—
Al in thy grace I put my fare.

The fresshe beautee of thy comlyhede[+]
32   So hote sette myn herte on fyr,
Whan I saw first thy maydenhede,
   That evere sith swich desire
Have I had to serve thee
36   Whil I may tire;
    That evere sith wyth cold of hete,
    Wyth hete of cold myn herte is bete,
    I nam but deed but thou me hete[+]
40   Thy love ageyn to quite my hire.

From which thou mayst me releve,
   Wolde thou vouchesauf to do so,
And from alle sores myn herte reve,[+]
44   Wyth a goodly word or two;

30. *I* not in MS.
31. **comlyhede** beauty, fairness
39. **hete** promise, assure
43. **reve** take away, separate

Myghte I fele in word or other
  That thou wast not my fo.
    In world a wight a thousand dele
48   Was nevere sonner+ broght to hele,
    For and thou lovede me trewely lele+
  Wolde I nevere have joyes mo.

Fairest of faire, this lettre lite,
52   That chief is of my peynes smerte
  (Al can I not wel endite),—
    Lat thise wordes synke in thyn herte.
For al my wele and wo, y-wis,
56   Thus I conclude in wordes shorte;
    But if thou rewe upon my peyne
    And brynge my bale to blisse ageyn,
    Certes I can not elles seyn
60   But deeth I may not a-sterte.+

48. **sonner** sooner
49. **lele** loyally, faithfully
57. *rewe* for MS. *rued*
60. **a-sterte** escape

77

Farewel, this world! I take my leve for evere,—
I am arested to appere at Goddes face.
O myghtyful God, thou knowest that I hadde levere +
4 Thanne al this world to have oon houre space
To make asseth + for al my grete trespas.
Myn herte, allas, is broken for that sorwe!
Som ben this day that shullen not ben to-morwe.

8 This lyf, I see, is but a chery-feire, + —
Alle thynges passen and so moot I algate. +
To-day I sat ful royal in a chaire
Til subtil Deeth knokked at my yate +
12 And unavysed he seyde to me, "Chekmat!"
Lo! how subtil he maketh a divors,
And wormes to fede he hath heer leyd my cors. +

Speketh softe, ye folk, for I am leyd a-sleep,—
16 I have my dreem, in trust is muche tresoun.
From Dethes hold + fayne wolde I make a leep,
But my wysdom is turned into feble resoun.
I see this worldes joye lasteth but a sesoun:

Index 769. Trin. Coll. Camb. MS. 1157, with readings from
Balliol Coll. Oxf. MS. 354. (*RL XV* No. 149.)
One other partial text. Fifteenth century.

3. **I hadde levere** I would rather, I would more willingly
5. **asseth** amends, expiation
8. **lyf . . . is but a chery-feire** life is transitory
9. **algate** in any case, at any rate
11. **yate** gate
14. **cors** corpse
17. **hold** stronghold; captivity

20 Wolde to God I hadde remembred me biforn!
　　I seye namore but be war of an horn.⁺

　　This feble world, so fals and so unstable,
　　Promoteth his lovers for a litel while;
24 But atte laste he yeveth hem a bable,⁺
　　Whan his peynted⁺ trouthe is turned into gile.
　　Experience causeth me the trouthe to compile,
　　Thenkyng this, to late, allas! that I bigan,
28 For folye and hope disceiven many a man.

　　Farewel, my frendes! The tide abideth no man,—
　　I moot departe hennes, and so shullen ye;
　　But in this passage the beste song that I can
32 Is *Requiem Eternum*—I preye God graunte it me.
　　Whan I have ended al myn adversitee,
　　Graunte me in paradys to have a mansioun,
　　That shedde his blood for my redempcioun.

21. **horn** i.e., the summons to Judgment
24. **bable** bauble, plaything
25. **peynted** pretended, disguised

78

In what estat+ so evere I be,
Timor mortis conturbat me.+

As I went in a myrie morwenynge
I herde a brid bothe wepe and synge;
This was the tenour+ of hir talkynge—
4   *Timor mortis conturbat me.*

I axed that brid what she mente.
"I am a musket+ bothe faire and gent;
For drede of deeth I am al shent:+
8   *Timor mortis conturbat me.*

"Whan I shal deye I knowe no day,
What contree or place I can not seye;
Wher-fore this song synge I may—
12   *Timor mortis conturbat me.*

"Jhesu Crist, whan he sholde deye,
To his Fader he gan seye,
'Fader,' he seyde, 'in trinitee,
16   *Timor mortis conturbat me.'*

Index 375. MS. Eng. poet. e. I. (*EEC* No. 370.)
Two other partial texts. *c.* 1470.

estat circumstance, condition, estate
Timor mortis conturbat me Fear of death distresses me
3. tenour substance, purport
6. musket (male) sparrowhawk
7. shent rendered useless, brought to ruin

"Alle cristen peple biholde and see
This world is but a vanytee,
And repleet wyth necessitee.
20 *Timor mortis conturbat me.*

"Wake I or slepe, ete or drynke,
Whan I on my laste ende do thenke,
For greet fere⁺ my soule doth shrynke:
24 *Timor mortis conturbat me.*"

God graunte us grace Him for-to serve,
And be at oure ende whan we sterve,⁺
And from the feend He us preserve!
28 *Timor mortis conturbat me.*

23. **fere** fear
26. **sterve** die

79

Evermore, wher-so-evere I be,
The drede of deeth doth trouble me.

As I went me for-to solace[+]
I herde a man sike and seye, "Allas,
Of me now thus stondeth the cas:
4   The drede of deeth doth trouble me.

"I have ben lord of tour and toun;
I sette noght by my grete renoun,
For deeth wol plukke it al adoun:
8   The drede of deeth doth trouble me.

"Whan I shal deye I am not seur,
In what contree or in what houre;
Wher-for I sobbyng seye to my power,
12   'The drede of deeth doth trouble me.'

"Whan my soule and my body departed[+] shullen be,
Of my juggement no man can telle me,
Nor of my place wher that I shal be:
16   Ther-fore drede of deeth doth trouble me.

"Jhesu Crist, whan that he sholde suffre his passioun,
To his Fader he seyde wyth greet devocioun,
'This is the cause of my intercessioun:
20   The drede of deeth doth trouble me.'

Index 376. MS. Eng. poet. e. I. (*EEC* No. 371.)
Unique text. *c.* 1470.

1. **me . . . solace** delight, amuse myself
7. *adoun* for MS. *downe*
13. **departed** divided, separated

"Alle cristen peple, beth ye wyse and ware,—
This world is but a chery-feire,[+]
Repleet wyth sorwe and fulfilled wyth care:
24   Ther-fore the drede of deeth doth trouble me.

"Whether that I be myrie or good wyne drynke,
Whan that I do on my laste day thenke,
It maketh my soule and body to shrynke,
28   For the drede of deeth sore troubleth me."

Jhesu us graunte Him so to honoure
That at oure ende He may be oure socour
And kepe us from the fendes power,
32   For than drede of deeth shal not trouble me.

22. **This world is but a chery-feire** i.e., The things of this world are transient

80

Care awey, awey, awey,
Care awey for evermore!

Al that I may swynke[+] or swete,
My wyf it wyl bothe drynke and ete;
If I seye aught she wyl me bete—
4   Care-ful is myn herte ther-for!

If I seye aught of hire but good,
She loketh on me as she were wood,
And wyl me cloute[+] aboute the hood—
8   Care-ful is myn herte ther-for!

If she wyl to the gode ale ride,
Me moste[+] trotte al by hir side;
And whan she drynketh I moot abide—
12   Care-ful is myn herte ther-for!

If I seye, "It shal be thus,"
She seyth, "Thou lyest, cherl, y-wus![+]
Wenestow[+] to overcome me thus?"
16   Care-ful is myn herte ther-for!

Index 210. MS. Eng. poet. e. I. (*SL XIV-XV* No. 44.)
Unique text. *c.* 1470.

1. **swynke** labor
3. *If* for MS. *&*.
7. **cloute** hit, clout
10. **me moste** I must
14. **y-wus** = *y-wis*
15. **wenestow** do you imagine (expect)

If any man have swich a wyf to lede,+
He shal knowe how *iudicare* cam in the crede;+
Of his penaunce God do him mede!
20   Care-ful is myn herte ther-for!

17. **lede** deal with
18. **how iudicare cam in the crede.** "The meaning here seems to be that
the husband is undergoing a 'hell on earth,' and that this punishment
should be credited him!" (*SL XIV-XV*, p. 240)

81

A, a, a, a,
Yet I love wher-so I go.

In al this world nis a murier lyf
Thanne is a yong man wythouten a wyf,
For he may lyven wythouten strif
4   In every place wher-so he go.

In every place he is loved over alle
Among maydens grete and smale—
In daunsyng, in pipyng, and rennyng at the balle,+
8   In every place wher-so he go.

They leten lighte by+ housebonde-men
Whan they at the balle renne;
They casten her love to yonge men
12   In every place wher-so they go.

Than seyn maydens, "Farewel, Jakke,
Thy love is pressed al in thy pak;
Thou berest thy love bihynde thy bak,
16   In every place wher-so thou go."

Index 1468. MS. Eng. poet. e. I. (*SL XIV-XV* No. 8.)
Unique text. *c.* 1470.

7. **rennyng at the balle** stool ball, probably, "played by men and women,
a simple game resembling cricket" (*SL XIV-XV*, p. 230)
9. **leten lighte by** think little of

82

Bryng us in good ale, and bryng us in good ale!
For oure blessed Ladies sake, bryng us in good ale!

Bryng us in no broun breed, for that is made of bren,
Nor bryng us in no white breed, for ther-inne is no game—
    But bryng us in good ale.

4   Bryng us in no beef, for there is many bones,
But bryng us in good ale, for that goth doun at ones—
    And bryng us in good ale.

Bryng us in no bacoun, for that is passyng fat,
8   But bryng us in good ale, and yif us ynough of that—
    And bryng us in good ale.

Bryng us in no moton, for that is ofte lene,
Nor bryng us in no trypes, for they ben selden clene—
12   But bryng us in good ale.

Bryng us in no eyren,[+] for ther are many shelles,
But bryng us in good ale, and yif us no thyng elles—
    And bryng us in good ale.

16   Bryng us in no butter, for ther-inne are many heres,
Nor bryng us in no pigges flessh, for that wyl make us
        bores—
    But bryng us in good ale.

Index 549. MS. Eng poet. e. I. (*SL XIV-XV* No. 13.)
One other (shorter) text. *c.* 1470.

13. **eyren** eggs

Bryng us in no podynges, for ther-inne is al gotes blood,
20 Nor bryng us in no venysoun, for that is not for oure good—
　　But bryng us in good ale.

Bryng us in no capons flessh, for that is often dere, +
Nor bryng us in no dokes flessh, for they slobere in the mere,
24 But bryng us in good ale.

20-21. *gotes blood* for MS. *Godes good*; *oure good* for MS. *owr blod*
22. **dere** costly, expensive

83

Nowel, el, el, el, el!
I thonke it a mayden everydel.

The firste day whan Crist was born,
Ther sprong a rose out of a thorn
To save mankynde that was forlorn:
4   I thonke it a mayden everydel.

In an oxe-stall that child was founde;
In poure clothyng the child was wounde;
He suffred many a deedly wounde:
8   I thonke it a mayden everydel.

A gerlond of thornes on his hed was set,
A sharp spere to his herte was smyt;
The Jewes seyde, "Tak thou that!"
12   I thonke it a mayden everydel.

The Jewes dide crien + her parlement,
On the day of juggement;
They weren aferd they sholde ben shent: +
16   I thonke it a mayden everydel.

Index 3344. MS. Eng. poet. e. I. (*EEC* No. 41.)
Unique text. *c.* 1470.

13. **dide crien** gave public, oral announcement (for the purpose of summoning)
15. **shent** ruined, brought to nothing. *ben* replaces MS. *hem.*

To the piler he was bounde,
To his herte a spere was stongen;
For us he suffred a deedly wounde:
20   I thonke it a mayden everydel.

18. *stongen* (MS. *stunggyn*) provides neither sense nor rhyme; possibly
the line should read: *His herte was stongen to the grounde* (**grounde**
base, bottom).

84

Of a rose, a lovely rose,
Of a rose I synge a song.

Lythe⁺ and listneth, bothe olde and yinge,⁺
How the rose bigan to sprynge;
A fairer rose to oure likyng
4   Sprong ther nevere in kynges lond.

Five braunches of that rose ther ben,
The which ben bothe faire and shene;
Of a mayden, Mary, hevene quene,
8   Out of hir bosom the braunche sprong.

The firste braunche was of greet honour,
That blessed Mary sholde bere the flour;
Ther cam an aungel out hevene tour
12   To breke the develes bond.

The seconde braunche was greet of myght
That sprong upon Cristemasse nyght;
The sterre shon and lemed⁺ bright
16   That man sholde see it bothe day and nyght.

Index 1914. MS. Eng. poet. e. I. (*EEC* No. 175A.)
Also in MS. Sloane 2593 and Balliol Coll. Oxf. MS. 354. *c.* 1470.

1. **Lythe** listen (imperative plural); **yinge** = *yonge;* **olde and yinge**
i.e., everybody
15. **lemed** shone, gleamed

The thridde braunche gan sprynge and sprede;
The kynges than the braunche gan lede
Tho to Oure Lady in hir child-bed,—
20   Into Bethleem that braunche sprong right.

The ferthe braunche, it sprong to helle
The develes power for-to felle,
That no soule ther-in sholde dwelle,
24   The braunche so blessedfully sprong.

The fifte braunche, it was so swote,+
It sprong to hevene bothe crop and rote+
In every bale to ben oure boot,
28   So blessedly it sprong.

18. *the* for MS. *to*
25. **swote** = *swete*
26. **crop and rote** top and root, i.e., entirely

85

Of alle the enemies that I can fynde
The tonge is most enemy to mankynde.

Wyth pitee moved I am constreyned
　　To synge a song for youre confort,
How that diverse have compleyned
4　　Of tonge untrewe and il report,
　　Seying thus wythoute desport:—

This tonge is instrument of discord,
　　Causyng werre and greet distaunce+
8　Bitwene the subjet and the lord,
　　The parfit cause of every grevaunce;
　　Wher-for I synge wythoute displesaunce:—

Thogh that prestes ben nevere so pacient
12　　In toun, citee, or in court royal,
Thogh the religious+ ben nevere so obedient,
　　Yet an il tonge wyl trouble hem alle;
　　Wher-for this song reherce I shal:—

16　If he that ille by another do seye
　　His propre fautes wolde biholde,
How ofte-tymes him-self were out of the wey,
　　Silence to him than sholde ben gold,
20　　And wyth me to synge he wolde ben bold:—

Index 4198. MS. Eng. poet. e. I. (*EEC* No. 342.)
Unique text. *c.* 1470.

7. **distaunce** quarreling
13. **religious** i.e., those in religious orders

148

From this tonge, a venymous serpent,
  Defend us, Fader, to Thee we preye,
As Thou unto us thy Sone hast sent
24 For-to ben born this present day,
  Lest that we synge and evermore seye:

Of alle the enemies that I can fynde
The tonge is most enemy to mankynde.

86

Sodeynly affrayed, half wakyng, half slepyng,
And greetly dismayde, a womman sat wepyng.

Wyth favour in hir face fer passyng my resoun,
And of hir sore wepyng this was the enchesoun: +
Hir sone in hir lappe lay, she seyde, slayn by tresoun.
4 If wepyng myghte ripe ben, it semed than in sesoun.
  "Jhesu!" so she sobbed,
   So hir sone was bobbed +
  And of his lyf robbed;
8 Seying thise wordes, as I seye thee:
"Who can not wepe, come lerne at me."

I seyde I coude not wepe, I was so hard-herted.
She answerde me wyth wordes shortely that smerted:
12 "Lo, nature shal meve + thee, thou most be converted.
Thyn owene fader this nyght is deed," lo, thus she
   thwarted, +
  "So my sone is bobbed
  And of his lyf robbed."
16   For sothe than I sobbed,
  Verifying the wordes she seyde to me:
Who can not wepe may lerne at thee.

Index 4189. John Rylands Library, Manchester. Lat. MS. 395.
(*RL XV* No. 9.)
One other text. Fifteenth century.

2. **enchesoun** reason, occasion
6. **bobbed** buffeted (and mocked)
12. **meve** move
13. **thwarted** retorted

"Now breek, herte, I thee preye! This cors lieth so rewely,+
20 So beten, so wounded, entreted+ so Jewely,+
What wight may me biholde and wepe not? Non, trewely,
To see my dede dere sone lie bledyng, lo, this newely."
      Ay stille she sobbed
24   So hir sone was bobbed
      And of his lyf robbed,
Newyng the wordes, as I seye thee:
"Who can not wepe, come lerne at me."

28 On me she caste hir eye, seyde, "See, man, thy brother!"
She kiste him and seyde, "Swete, am I not thy moder?"
In swownyng she fil ther, it wolde be non other.
I not+ which more deedly, that oon or that other.
32   Yet she revived and sobbed
      So hir sone was bobbed
      And of his lyf robbed.
"Who can not wepe"—this was the laye+—
36 And wyth that word she vanisht awey.

19. **rewely** ruefully, pitiably
20. **entreted** treated, dealt with; **Jewely** like a Jew
30. *swownyng* for MS. *sownyng*
31. **not** = *ne wot* know not
35. **laye** strain, purport

87

I wende to deeth, knight stith in stour,[+]
Thurgh fight in feeld I wan the flour;
No fightes me taughte the deeth to quelle—
4 I wende to deeth, sooth I you telle.

I wende to deeth, a kyng, y-wis;
What helpeth honour and worldes blisse?
Deeth is to man the kynde weye—
8 I wende to be cladde in cley.

I wende to deeth, clerk[+] ful of skile,
That coude wyth word men marre and dile;[+]
Soon has me made the deeth an ende—
12 Beth war wyth me! to deeth I wende.

Index 1387. Cotton MS. Faustina B.vi, Part II. (*RL XV* No. 158A.)

Two other texts. Fifteenth century.

1. **stith in stour** stout in battle
4. First *I* not in MS.
9. **clerk** one in religious orders
10. **marre and dile** bewilder and assuage; ruin and conceal

88

Al worldly welthe passed me fro;
Nunc in pulvere dormio.+

I hadde richesse, I hadde my helthe,
I hadde honour and worldly welthe;
Yet deeth hath take me hennes by stelthe.
4   *Nunc in pulvere dormio.*

Of al solas+ I hadde my wylle,
Of mete and drynke having my fille;
Yet deeth hath smyt me wyth his bille.+
8   *Nunc in pulvere dormio.*

I hadde beautee in hond and face,
I hadde confort in every cas;
Yet, arested wyth dethes mace,
12   *Nunc in pulvere dormio.*

I hadde musik, I hadde swete song,
And other game and myrthe among;
Yet deeth hath felled my wyth his prong.
16   *Nunc in pulvere dormio.*

I hadde connyng, wysdom, and wyt;
Manhod and strengthe in me were knit;
Yet deeth hath broght me to my pit.+
20   *Nunc in pulvere dormio.*

Index 1298. Camb. Univ. MS. Ee. I. 12. (*EEC* No. 353.)
Unique text. By James Ryman. *c.* 1490.

Nunc in pulvere dormio Now I sleep in dust
5. **solas** amusement, pleasure
7. **bille** instrument for pruning or cutting; sword, ax
19. **pit** grave

O man, which art erthe by thy kynde,
Whos lyf is but a blast of wynd,
This dredeful word bere in thy mynde:
24   *"Nunc in pulvere dormio."*

Whil thou art heer, man, wel thee gide,
For thou shalt not ay heer abide;
But thou shalt seye, man, at a tide:
28   *"Nunc in pulvere dormio."*

Almyghty God, graunte us alle grace
Wel to expende oure tyme and space
Er-that we come unto that cas.
32   *Nunc in pulvere dormio.*

89

Mary hath born allone
The Sone of God in trone.[+]

That mayden mylde hir child dide kepe
   As modres don echoon,
But hir dere Sone ful sore dide wepe
4   For synful man allone.

She rokked Him and song "Lullay,"
   But evere He made greet mone;
"Dere Sone," she seyde, "tel, I thee preye,
8   Why Thou dost wepe allone."

"Moder," He seyde, "I shal be slayn,
   That synne dide nevere non,
And suffre deeth wyth woful peyne,—
12   Ther-fore I wepe allone."

"Lullay," she seyde, "sleep and be stille,
   And lat be al thy mone;
For al thyng is at thyn owene wylle
16   In hevene and erthe allone."

"Moder," He seyde, "how sholde I slepe?
   How sholde I leve my mone?
I have more cause to sobbe and wepe
20   Sith I shal deye allone."

Index 3284. Camb. Univ. MS. Ee. I. 12. (*EEC* No. 154.)
Unique text. By James Ryman. *c.* 1490.

trone throne

"Dere Sone," she seyde, "the Kyng of Blisse,
   That is so heighe in trone,
Knoweth that Thou didest nevere amys—
24   Why sholdest thou deye allone?"

"Moder," He seyde, "only of thee
   I took bothe flessh and bon
To save mankynde and make it free
28   Wyth myn herte blood allone."

"Dere Sone," she seyde, "Thou art equal
   To God, that is in trone;
For man, ther-fore, that is so thral, +
32   Why sholdest Thou deye allone?"

"Moder," He seyde, "my Faders wylle
   And myn they ben but oon;
Ther-fore by skile + I moot fulfille
36   My Faders wylle allone."

"Dere Sone," she seyde, "sith Thou hast take
   Of me bothe flessh and bon,
If it may be, me not forsak
40   In care and wo allone."

"For man I moot the raunsoun paye,
   The which to helle is gon,
Moder," He seyde, "on Good Friday,
44   For he may not allone."

"Dere Sone," she seyde unto Him tho,
   "Whan Thou from me art gon,
Than shal I lyve in care and wo
48   Wythoute confort allone."

31. **thral** enslaved
35. **skile** reason

"Moder," He seyde, "tak thou no thoght—
  For me mak thou no mone;
Whan I have boght that I have wroght
52   Thou shalt not be allone.

"On the thridde day, I thee bihighte, +
  After that I am gon,
I wol arise by my grete myght
56   And conforte thee allone."

49. *thoght* for MS. *nought*
53. **bihighte** promise

90

Sancta Maria, ora pro nobis.[+]

O Moder mylde, Mayde undefiled,
That we so wilde[+] be not bigiled
   And evere exiled from Crist and his,
4   *Ora pro nobis.*

O Quene of grace, moste faire of face,
Of al solas ledyng the trace,[+]
   Of that heighe place that we not mysse,
8   *Ora pro nobis.*

O Lady free, of heighe degree,
That we mowen see thy Sone and thee
   And evere to be wher al joye is,
12   *Ora pro nobis.*

That Crist us sende grace to amende
Oure tyme myspent er we hennes wende,[+]
   And at oure ende to graunte us blisse,
16   *Ora pro nobis.*

Index 2527. Camb. Univ. MS. Ee. I. 12. (*EEC* No. 220.)
Unique text. By James Ryman. *c.* 1490.

   Sancta Maria, ora pro nobis Saint Mary, pray for us
2. **wilde** wayward, unsubmitting
6. **ledyng the trace** at the forefront of a line or procession, i.e., excelling,
   exceeding
14. **hennes wende** turn (go) hence, i.e., die

91

Revert, revert, revert, revert!
O synful man, yif me thyn herte.

Have mynde how I mankynde[+] have take
Of a pure mayde, man, for thy sake,
That were most bounde most free to make.
4 O synful man, yif me thyn herte.

Have mynde, thou synful creature,
I took baptesme in thy nature
From filthe of synne to make thee pure.
8 O synful man, yif me thyn herte.

Have mynde, man, how I took the feeld,
Upon my bak beryng my sheeld;
For peyne ne deeth I wolde not yelde.
12 O synful man, yif me thyn herte.

Have mynde, I was put on the rode
And for thy sake shedde myn herte blood;
Bihold my peyne—bihold my mood!
16 O synful man, yif me thyn herte.

Bihold me, hed, hond, foot, and side!
Bihold my woundes five so wide!
Bihold the peyne that I abide!
20 O synful man, yif me thyn herte.

Index 1125. Camb. Univ. MS. Ee. I. 12. (*EEC* No. 269.)
Unique text. By James Ryman. *c.* 1490.

1. **mankynde** i.e., human form

Have mynde, man, how faste I was bounde
For thy sake to a piler rounde, +
Scourged til my blood fil to grounde.
24   O synful man, yif me thyn herte.

Have mynde how I in forme of breed
Have left my flessh and blood to wedde +
To make thee quik whan thou art deed.
28   O synful man, yif me thyn herte.

Have mynde, man, how I have thee wroght,
How wyth my blood I have thee boght,
And how to blisse I have thee broght.
32   O synful man, yif me thyn herte.

O synful man, bihold and see
What I have don and do for thee,
If thou wylt be in blisse wyth me.
36   O synful man, yif me thyn herte.

Bothe for my deeth and peynes smerte
That I suffred for thy desserte +
I axe namore, man, but thyn herte.
40   Revert, revert, revert, revert.

22. **rounde** (?) openly, without concealment
26. **to wedde** as a pledge
38. **desserte** desert, i.e., what mankind deserved

92

O man unkynde,
Have thou in mynde
My passioun smerte!
4 Thou shalt me fynde
To thee ful kynde:
Lo, heer myn herte.

Index 2507. Trinity Coll. Camb. MS. 1157. (Henry A. Person, *Cambridge Middle English Lyrics*, 2d ed., No. 9.)
Two other texts. Fifteenth century.

93

Ther bloweth a cold wynd to-day, to-day,
  The wynd bloweth cold to-day;
Crist suffred his passioun for mannes salvacioun
  To kepe the colde wynd awey.

This wynd by resoun is called temptacioun—
  It raveth bothe nyght and day;
Remembre, man, how thy Saveour was slawen
4   To kepe the colde wynd awey.

Pride and presumpcioun and fals extorcioun
  That many man don bitraye—
Man, com to contricioun and axe confessioun
8   To kepe the colde wynd awey.

O Mary mylde, for love of thy child
  That deyde on Good Friday,
Be oure salvacioun from mortal dampnacioun
12   To kepe the colde wynd awey.

He was nayled, his blood was haled,[+]
  Oure remissioun for-to beye,
And for oure synnes alle He drank bothe eisel[+] and galle
16   To kepe the colde wynd awey.

Index 3525. MS. Ashmole 1379. (*EEC* No. 170.)
Unique text. *c.* 1500.

9. *thy* for MS. *the*
13. **haled** caused to flow (in a large stream)
15. **eisel** vinegar

Slouthe, envye, covetise, and lechery
   Blewe the colde wynd, as I dar seye;
Ayeins swich poyson He suffred his passioun
20   To kepe the colde wynd awey.

O man, remembre the Lord so tendre
   Which deyde wythouten denay;
His hondes so smerte laye next to his herte
24   To kepe the colde wynd awey.

Now preye we alle to the kyng celestial,
   That born He was of may,
That we mowen love so wyth othere mo
28   To kepe the colde wynd awey.

At the day of doom whan we shullen come
   Oure synnes not for-to denaye,
Mary, preye to thy Sone that sightly is in trone⁺
32   To kepe the colde wynd awey.

At the laste ende, man, thou shalt sende
   And kepe bothe nyght and day;
The moste goodliest tresour is Crist the Saveour
36   To kepe the colde wynd awey.

Heer lat us ende, and Crist us defende
   Al by the nyght and by day,
And brynge us to his place wher is myrthe and solas
40   To kepe the colde wynd awey.

31. **trone** throne. *thy* for MS. *the* and *is in* for MS. *yn hys*

94

Allone, allone, allone, allone, allone—
Heer I sitte allone, allas! allone.

As I walked me this endre day
To the grene-wode for-to pleye
And al hevynesse to putte awey,
4   My-self allone;—

As I walked under the grene-wode bough
I saw a mayde faire ynough;
A child she happed,⁺ she song, she lough,⁺—
8   That child wepede allone.

"Sone," she seyde, "I have Thee born
To save mankynde that was forlorn;
Ther-fore I preye Thee, Sone, ne murne,
12   But be stille allone."

"Moder, me thinketh it is right ille
That men me sechen for-to spille,⁺
For hem to save it is my wylle;
16   Ther-fore I cam hider allone."

"Sone," she seyde, "lat it be in thy thoght,
For mannes gilt is not wyth-soght;⁺
For Thou art He that hath al wroght,
20   And I thy moder allone."

Index 364. B.M. Addit. MS. 5465. (*RL XV* No. 2.)
Unique text. *c.* 1500.

7. **happed** clasped, protected; **lough** laughed
14. **spille** destroy, kill; *me* not in MS.
18. **wyth-soght** pursued; *soght* for MS. *stone*

95

Who wot now that is heer
Wher he shal be another yeer?

Another yeer it may bitide
This companye to ben ful wide,
And nevere another heer to abide—
4   Crist may sende now swich a yeer.

Another yeer it may bifalle
The leste⁺ that is wythinne this halle
To ben more maister thanne we alle—
8   Crist may sende now swich a yeer.

Thise lordes that ben wonder grete,
They threten poure men for-to bete;
It lendeth litel⁺ in her threte—
12   Crist may sende now swich a yeer.

Index 320. B.M. Addit. MS. 40166(C3). (*EEC* No. 121.)
Unique text. Fifteenth century.

6. **The leste** The least, The lowliest (one)
11. **It lendeth litel** Little dwells, is contained
12. *now* not in MS.

96

Hey, ey, hey, ey,
Make we myrie as we may.+

Now is Yole+ comen wyth gentil chere—
Of myrthe and gamen he hath no pere;
In every lond wher he cometh nere
4   Is myrthe and gamen, I dar wel seye.

Now is comen a messager
Of thy lord, Sir Newe Yeer;
Biddeth us alle ben myrie heer
8   And make as myrie as we may.

Ther-fore every man that is heer
Synge a carole on his manere;
If he can non we shullen him lere,
12   So that we ben myrie alwey.

Whoso-evere maketh hevy chere,+
Were he nevere to me dere,
In a dich+ I wolde he were
16   To drye his clothes til it were day.

Mende the fyr and make good chere!
Fill the cuppe, sire boteler!
Lat every man drynke to his fere!+
20   This endeth my carole wyth care awey.

Index 2343. B.M. Addit. MS. 14997. (*SL XIV-XV* No. 3.)
Unique text. 1500.

may = *mowen*
1. **Yole** Yuletide
13. **maketh hevy chere** is somber, causes unhappiness
15. **dich** ditch, moat
19. **fere** fellow, companion

97

Bon jour, bon jour a vous!
I am come unto this hous,
  Wyth par la pompe,[+] *I seye.*

Is ther any good man heer
That wyl make me any chere?
And if ther were I wolde come nere
4   To wite what he wolde seye.
      A! Wol ye ben wilde?[+]
      By Mary mylde,

    . . . .
8   I trowe ye wol synge gaye.

Beth gladly, maistres, everichoon!
I am come my-self allone
To appose[+] you oon by oon.
12   Lat see who dar seye nay.—
      Sire, what seye ye?[+]
      Syng on, lete us see.—
      Now wyl it be
16   This or another day?

Index 1609. Balliol Coll. Oxf. MS. 354. (*SL XIV-XV* No. 1.)
Unique text. *c.* 1500.

    par la pompe with ceremonial celebration, procession
 5. **wilde** wayward, uncooperative
11. **appose** interrogate, examine
13. **seye ye** = *seyst thou*

Lo, this is he that wyl don the dede:
He trempreth+ his mouth—ther-fore tak hede—
Syng softe, I seye, lest thy nose blede,
20   For hurte thy-self thou may.+
          But by God that me boghte,
          Thy brest is so toght,+
          Til thou hast wel coughed
24   Thou mayst not ther-wyth awey.

Sire, what seyst thou wyth thy face so lene?
Thou syngest neither good tenour, treble, ne mene.
Utter not thy vois wythoute thy brest be clene,
28   Hertely I thee preye!
          I holde thee excused,
          Thou shalt be refused,
          For thou hast not ben used
32   To no good sport ne pleye.

Sire, what seyst thou wyth thy fat face?
Me thinketh thou sholdest bere a very good base
To a pot of good ale or ypocras,+
36   Trewely as I thee seye!
          Hold up thy hed,
          Thou lokest like leed;
          Thou wastest muche breed
40   Evermore from day to day.

18. **trempreth** makes ready
20. **thou may** = *thou mayst*
22. **toght** taut, pressed tight; congested
35. **ypocras** spiced wine, a cordial

Now wol ye see wher he stondeth bihynde?
Y-wis, brother, thou best unkynde!
Stond forth and waste wyth my som wynd,
44   For thou hast ben called a synger ay.
        Nay, be not ashamed,
        Thou shalt not be blamed,
        For thou hast ben famed
48   The worst in this contree!

98

Make we myrie bothe more and lasse[+]
For now is the tyme of Cristemasse.

Lat no man come into this halle—
Grome, page, nor yet marchal[+]—
But that som sport[+] he brynge wyth-al,
4   For now is the tyme of Cristemasse.

If that he seye he can noght synge,
Som other sport than lat him brynge
That it may plese at this festeyinge,[+]
8   For now is the tyme of Cristemasse.

If he seye he can noght do,
Than for my love axe him no mo,
But to the stokkes than lat him go,
12   For now is the tyme of Cristemasse.

Index 1866. Balliol Coll. Oxf. MS. 354. (*SL XIV-XV* No. 2.)
Unique text. *c.* 1500.

  lasse = *lesse*
2. **marchal** marshal (for ceremonial occasion)
3. **sport** amusement, entertainment (disport)
7. **festeyinge** feasting

99

Lully, lullay, lully, lullay,
The faucon+ hath born my make awey.

He bar him up, he bar him down,
He bar him into an orchard broun.

In that orchard ther was an halle
4   That was hanged wyth purpre and palle.+

And in that halle ther was a bed,
It was hanged wyth gold so red.

And in that bed ther lieth a knight,
8   His woundes bledyng day and nyght.

By that beddes side ther kneleth a may,
And she wepeth bothe nyght and day.

And by that beddes side ther stondeth a ston,
12   *Corpus Cristi* writen ther-on.

Index 1132. Balliol Coll. Oxf. MS. 354. (*EEC* No. 322A.)
Three traditional versions recorded in nineteenth century.
c. 1500.

faucon falcon
4. **purpre and palle** rich and fine (purple) cloth

100

For wele or wo I wyl not flee
To love that herte that loveth me.

That herte myn herte hath in swich grace
   That of two hertes oon herte make we;
That herte hath broght myn herte in cas
4   To love that herte that loveth me.

For oon that like unto that herte
   Nevere was nor is nor nevere shal be,
Nor nevere like cause sette this aparte
8   To love that herte that loveth me;

Which cause yeveth cause to me and myn
   To serve that herte of soverayntee,
And stille to synge this lattere lyne:
12   To love that herte that loveth me.

What-evere I seye, what-evere I synge,
   What-evere I do, that herte shal see
That I shal serve wyth herte lovynge
16   That lovynge herte that loveth me.

This knotte thus knyt who shal untwyne,
   Sith we that knytte it don agree
To lose ne slyppe, but bothe enclyne
20   To love that herte that loveth me?

Index 3271. Canterbury Cathedral: Christ Church Letters, Vol.
  II, No. 174. (*EEC* No. 444.)
Unique text. *c.* 1500.

Farewel, of hertes that herte most fyn,
Farewel, dere herte, hertely to thee,
And kepe this herte of myn for thyn
24   As herte for herte for lovyng me.

SELECTED FRAGMENTS

Swete lemman, thyn ore!

(LLME, p. 174)

At the wrastlyng my lemman I ches, [chose]
And at the ston-castyng I him for-les. [lost]

(LLME, p. 174)

Than crewen cokkes
And than was it day.

(LLME, p. 181)

Have good day, my lemman!

(LLME, p. 188)

Giveth me no gerlond of grene
But it be of withins i-wroght. [willow branches]

(LLME, p. 188)

Com hider, love, to me!

(LLME, p. 188)

I have loved so many a day,
Lightly sped, but bettre I may.

This endre day whan me was wo
Nyghtengale to move me to
Under a bough ther I lay . . . .

(LLME, p. 180)

Brid on brere I telle it to—
Non other I ne dar.

(LLME, p. 181)

Joly shepherd of Asshel-doun
Can more on love thanne al this toun.

(*EEL*, p. 279)

I come hider to wowe . . . .

(*LLME*, p. 189)

The ship saileth over the salte fom
Wyl brynge her marchantz and my lemman hom.

(*LLME*, p. 189)

Princesse of youthe and flour of godlihede,
The parfite mirour of al gentilesse.

(*LLME*, p. 178)

My love she murneth for me, for me,
My love she murneth for me.

(*LLME*, p. 182)

Amonges alle myrthes many
We shullen synge of oon lady—
In al this world nis swich a sight.

(*LLME*, p. 183)

I am not unkynde
To love as I fynde . . . .

(*LLME*, p. 190)

Lie thou me neer, lemman,
In thyne armes . . . .

(*LLME*, p. 190)

GLOSSARY

Words glossed on the same page on which they occur in the poems are not listed below, unless (1) they have been assigned specialized meanings in specific texts but occur elsewhere with more usual meanings; or (2) it is convenient to list the inflectional forms in one place, in the Glossary. (See the Introduction, page xv.)

Inflectional forms of nouns, adjectives, and verbs are given when necessary. Unlabeled principal parts of verbs are to be understood as preterite singular and past participle if two forms appear in parentheses following the headword, and as preterite singular, preterite plural, and past participle if three forms appear.

adrede(n) fear, be afraid

afore, aforn before, beforehand, formerly

al (adj. and noun) pl. **alle** all, every; everything

al (adv.) entirely, very, quite, wholly

also (adv.) also, equally, similarly; as (conj.) as, as if
  also soon as soon as

amende(n) to make better, improve, make amends, set right

axe(n) ask, inquire; require

ay always, ever, continually, on every occasion

ayeins against

bad *see* **bidde(n)**

bale torment, misery, misfortune, sorrow

bar *see* **bere(n)**

be(n) to be Pr. sg. 1 **am**, 2 **art, best,** 3 **is, beth**; pl. **ben, beth**; subj. sg. **be**, pl. **ben**. Pt. sg. 1, 3 **was**, 2 **were, wast**; pl. **were(n)**; subj. sg. **were**, pl. **were(n)**. Ppl. **ben, i-be.** Imp. sg. **be**, pl. **beth.**

bere(n) (**bar, beren, born**) to bear, carry, possess, hold; give birth to

best best. *See also* **be(n)**

beste (noun) beast, animal, creature

bete(n) (**bette, bete(n)**) to beat, scourge

beye(n) (**boghte, boght**) to buy, pay for, redeem

bidde(n) (**bad, bidden**) to pray, ask, bid; offer; command, direct

bifore, biforn before

bihete(n) (**bihete, bihote**) to promise

biknowe(n) to acknowledge, confess; recognize

bileve (noun) belief, faith

bille letter, note

biseche(n) (**bisoghte, bisoght**) to beseech, entreat, implore

bisee(n) to attend to, give heed to

bisynesse activity; preoccupation; care, anxiety

177

bithenke(n) (bithoghte, bithoght) to reflect, bethink, consider, concern oneself

bitide(n) to happen, befall

blisse happiness, bliss, joy

blithe happy, glad, blithe

blosme blossom, flower

blynne(n) to cease, cease from

bon bone

boon boon, request, prayer

bour abode, dwelling-place; bower, chamber

breed bread

breke(n) (brak, breken, broken) to break

brenne(n) to burn

brid (young) bird

burde maiden

can (pr. pl. **conne**) to know, understand; be able, know how to, can

cas circumstance, case; affair; condition, plight

chere face, appearance, demeanor; (good) **cheer**

clene clean, pure; splendid
  clennesse cleanness, purity

clepe(n) to call, name, summon; mention

come(n) (cam, comen, comen) to come

conne *see* **can**

cosse kiss

dar (inf. **durre(n)**, pt. **durste**) to dare

dayesyes daisies

debonaire, deboner gracious, courteous; of good disposition

dede deed, event, act

deed (adj. and noun) pl. **dede** dead

deeth death

dele(n) to deal, allot, distribute, deal with, perform

demened (ppl. adj.) conducted, managed, expressed

dere (adj.) dear, beloved, valued; (adv.) dearly

deye(n) to die

disese discomfort, distress, misery, sorrow

do(n) to do, cause, act, make. Also as preterite auxiliary form
  do(n) wey set aside, do away with, abolish

domes-day the Day of Judgment

doom judgment, decision

drawe(n) (drough, drawen) to draw, pull; bring; add

drede fear

drough *see* **drawe(n)**

ech each
  ech a every

eet *see* **ete(n)**

eke also, moreover

endite(n) to write, dictate or compose (for writing)

endre recent, just passed
  endre day a day or two ago

er comp. **erre** before, earlier, formerly. Also **er-than, er-that**

ete(n) (eet, eten) to eat

everich(a) every

everichoon everyone

everydel altogether, every bit, in every part

eye pl. **eyen** eye

falle(n) (fil, fallen) to fall

fame fame, reputation; rumor; report

fare(n) (for, foren, faren) to go, fare; behave, conduct

faute fault
fautles faultless
fay, fey faith
fayn glad; eager, willing. Also
  adverb
feend pl. **fendes** devil, the Devil;
  foe
fer far
fey *see* **fay**
feyne(n) to feign, pretend
fil *see* **falle(n)**
flood pl. **flodes** flood, water,
  stream, sea
flour flower
fode food, sustenance
fond *see* **fynde(n)**
for *see* **fare(n)**
forlete(n) relinquish, give up entirely. *See also* **lete(n)**
forlorn (ppl. and adj.) lost; ruined,
  degraded
for-than because
for-thy therefore; because
founde(n) *see* **fynde(n)**
fowel bird
free noble, gracious, generous; free;
  forward, immodest
fro from
fynde(n) (**fond, founde(n),**
  founden) to find
fyr fire

game, gamen amusement; game,
  sport; merriment; joy, pleasure
gan (pt. of **gynne**) began, under-
  took (and carried out). Also a
  verb auxiliary indicating past
  time: did
gest guest
gilt guilt
glee pl. **glewes** mirth, pleasure;
  entertainment; music

go(n) to go, walk, move. Pr. sg. 1
  go, 2 **gost,** 3 **goth;** pl. **go(n);**
  subj. sg. **go,** pl. **go(n).** Pt.
  went. Ppl. **gon, i-go.** Imp.
  sg. **go,** pl. **goth**
gostly spiritual
grete(n) (pt. sg. 1, 3 **grette**) to
  greet
ground bottom, foundation, base,
  ground
gynne *see* **gan**

han *see* **have(n)**
hap chance, (good) fortune
have(n), han to have, possess, keep,
  get. Pr. sg. 1 **have,** 2 **havest,**
  hast, 3 **haveth, hath;** pl.
  have(n), han; subj. sg. **have,**
  pl. **have(n).** Pt. sg. 1, 3
  hadde, 2 **haddest,** pl.
  hadde(n); subj. sg. **hadde,**
  pl. **hadde(n).** Ppl. **had,**
  i-had. Imp. sg. **have,** pl.
  haveth
hed head
heer (1) here; (2) pl. **heres** hair
heighe (adj. and noun) high, noble.
  Also adverb
hele health; prosperity; restoration,
  recovery
hele(n) to heal, restore
hende (adj. and noun) gracious,
  courteous, gentle; pleasant
hennes hence
hente(n) to seize, obtain
herber arbor, garden, grassy place
  among trees
herbere(n) to harbor, protect
here(n) to hear, listen to
herie(n) to praise, worship; honor
herte heart
hevy heavy; sad

hewe hue, complexion, appearance, beauty
hond hand

ilke each, every; **that ilke** that same, that very (one)

kene bold, eager, keen; sharp; cruel
kepe(n) to keep, preserve, take care of
kyn, kynne kin, race, kind
kynde (noun) nature; (adj.) kind; natural

ladden *see* **lede(n)**
largesse generosity, liberality
lat *see* **lete(n)**
leche physician; means of recovery
lede(n) (**ledde, ladden, led / i-lad**) to lead, guide; direct; bring; pass
leef (1) (noun) pl. **leves** leaf; (2) (adj.) inflected **leve** dear, beloved; agreeable
  leefly dear, lovely
lemman beloved (one); lover, sweetheart
lenger (comp. of **longe**) longer
lere(n) to learn; teach
lese(n) (ppl. **i-lorn**) to lose
lete(n) (**lett, letten**) to let, allow, permit; leave, let go, relinquish; abandon, forsake. Also, **lat** as verb auxiliary indicating hortative mood
leve(n) to leave; abandon, neglect, forsake
leves *see* **leef**
light (noun and adj.) light
like(n) to please. Also in impersonal constructions: e.g., **thee liketh** it pleases you
  like ille to displease
likne(n) to liken, compare

liste(n) as impersonal verb, to desire, wish; be pleased; e.g., **thee list** it pleases you; **me listeth** it pleases me
lite, litel little, small
lore teaching, instruction; doctrine
(i-)lorn *see* **lese(n)**
loude loudly
lufsom (comp. **lufsomer**) lovesome; beautiful, lovely
lust pleasure, desire, delight; lust
lusty desirable, pleasant

make mate
  makeles without mate, matchless, peerless
mankynde, mankynne mankind
may (1) maiden; (2) pr. pl. **mowe(n)** may, can, be able, be permitted
mede reward, meed; bribe
meed (1) meadow; (2) mead (a drink)
mele meal, repast
mete food
mo more
moder mother
mone (1) complaint, lamentation, moan; (2) moon
mood mood, spirit, temper; thought; mind
moot (pr. sg. 1, 3, **moot**, 2 **most**, pl. **mote**; pt. **moste**) must; can; may
morwe morning, morrow; day
morwenynge morning
mowe *see* **may** (2)
muche, muchel much; great. Also adverb
murier, muriest *see* **myrie**
murne(n) to mourn, lament, sorrow
myddel middle; waist

myrie (murier, muriest) merry, gay, joyous, pleasant. Also adverb

myrthe joy, mirth; amusement; pleasure

myschief misfortune, distress, adversity

mysese discomfort; trouble, harm

namore (adj.) = *no more* no other, nothing more; (adv.) nevermore

ne a negative particle

neer *see* **nere**

neighe(n) to approach, near

nemne(n) to name, mention

nere (comp. neer) near

nis = *ne is*

noght (noun) nothing (at all); (adv.) not, not at all

nyl = *ne wyl*

o, oo ever, always

oon (pronoun) one (person, thing, etc.); (adj.) one, a single

    at ones once, on one (single) occasion

oone (adv.) alone, only

ore favor; grace; mercy

oth oath

other (adj.) second; other; (noun) others; (conj.) or

owene, owe (adj.) own

parfit perfect

pere equal, peer

peyne pain, distress, torment, suffering

pleye(n) to play, amuse oneself

pleying play, amusement, sport, entertainment

poure poor

preye(n) to pray; beseech

prike(n) to prick, cause to ache

pris worth, excellence, value; prize

prively privately, intimately

propre (adj.) own

pyne misery, torment, pain, grief

pyne(n) to (cause) torment, pain; cause misery, cause grief

ran *see* **renne(n)**

rede advice, counsel

    what shal me to rede what shall I do

rede(n) to advise, counsel

renne(n) (ran, ronne, ronne) to run, go; flow

reve(n) to bereave, take away; rob, plunder

rewe(n) to pity, have pity (for); rue, regret. Also in impersonal constructions: e.g., **me reweth** I have pity (or regret) for; **it reweth me** I regret, it causes me regret

reweful rueful, pitiable; sad, grievous

rode rood, cross

ronne *see* **renne(n)**

saw *see* **see(n)**

seche(n) (soghte, soght) to seek, search

see(n) (saw, sawen, seen) to see, perceive

seemly seemly, fair, becoming

sene manifest, visible

seur sure

seven-nyght seven nights; a week

seye(n), seyn to say; tell

shal (pr. pl. shullen) shall, will; am to (is to, etc.), ought to. Also as auxiliary verb

shene fair, shining, beautiful

shilde(n) to shield, protect; defend

shrynke(n) to wither, shrink
sik (1) (noun) sigh; (2) (adj.) sick
sike(n) to sigh; regret
siker (adj.) sure, certain, secure.
  Also as adverb
sith (adv. and conj.) afterward,
  after (that); since, after, when
    sithen afterward
    sith-that from the time that
slawen see slee(n)
slee(n) (ppl. slayn / slawen) to
  slay, strike down
so so; as
soghte see seche(n)
solas solace, consolation; comfort
somer springtime
sone son
song song. See also synge(n)
sonne sun
sooth (noun) (the) truth; (adj.)
  true
    for sothe forsooth, in truth,
      truly
sore (noun) pain, sore, misery;
  (adj.) sore, grievous, painful;
  (adv.) sorely, grievously, pain-
  fully; exceedingly
sorwe sorrow, grief, pain
sorwe(n) to grieve, (cause) sorrow
speke(n) to speak, talk
spray (small) branch, spray
sprynge(n) (sprong, sprongen)
  to spring; sprout, grow
stal see stele(n)
stark strong, powerful; severe
stele(n) (stal, stelen, stolen) to
  steal
sterre star
stinge(n) (ppl. stongen) to pierce;
  sting
stolen see stele(n)
stonde(n) to stand; remain
stongen see stinge(n)

stounde space of time, short time;
  moment; time of suffering
stour strong, stalwart
stout strong; proud; stately, mag-
  nificent
stynte(n) to stint, cease, stop
sustene(n) to sustain
swete (swetter, swettest) sweet;
  pleasant. Also as noun, sweet one,
  fair one
swetyng beloved, sweetheart, sweet
  one
swich such
swinge(n) (ppl. swongen) to
  strike, beat, whip
swithe very (much), exceedingly;
  quickly
synge(n) (song, songen, songen)
  to sing
synne sin

telle(n) to tell, recount; enumerate,
  count
tente intent, notice
tere (noun) tear
than then, thereupon; afterward;
  consequently
thanne than
that (demonstrative pronoun) pl.
  tho that, pl. those; (relative pronoun) that
thenke(n) (thoghte, thoght) to
  think, conceive, consider
thennes thence
this pl. thise this, pl. these
tho then. See also that
thoghte see thenke(n), thynke(n)
thole(n) to endure, suffer; be
  patient
thrynge(n) to press, thrust, make
  (one's) way
thurgh through; by means of;
  because of

thyng pl. **thyng / thynges** thing; pl. things, affairs, matters

thynke(n) (**thoghte, thoght**) impersonal verb, to seem (to)

tide time

togidre together

trowe(n) to believe, think

uncouth strange, foreign; unknown

under under, beneath; behind

variaunce inconstancy

wan pale, wan; dark

waxe(n) (**wex, wexen, waxen**) to wax, grow; become

wei woe

wel well; many, much; easily; good; very

wele happiness, good fortune, wealth, prosperity

wende(n) to turn, change; go (away), depart; pass

wene(n) to expect; suppose, imagine; think

wepe(n) to weep

werke(n) (ppl. **wroght**) to work, cause, make, bring about

werre war

whan when

whil (conj.) while

while (noun) a time, while

whilom formerly, once

wight wight, person, creature

wite(n) to know, learn; be aware, hold in mind. Pr. sg. 1, 3 **wot**, 2 **wost**; pl. **wiste**

wode wood, forest

wol, wollen *see* **wylle**

wone(n) to dwell, live; remain

wood mad

wot *see* **wite(n)**

wowe(n) to woo, make love

wroght *see* **werke(n)**

wrong (noun) wrong, injustice; (adj.) wrong, unjust
>   **wronge** (adv.) wrongfully, unjustly
>   **wyth wronge** wrongfully, unjustly

wroth angry

wyl, wylle will, desire; purpose

wylle to wish, desire, be willing. Also as auxiliary verb. Pr. sg. 1, 3 **wyl, wol**, 2 **wylt, wolt**; pl. **wol, wollen**. Pt. sg. **wolde**, pl. **wolde(n)**

wynne joy, bliss

wynne(n) to win, get, gain

yelde(n) to yield, produce; repay

yeve(n) (**yaf, yeven, yeven**) to give, grant

yift gift

yore a long time (ago), of old; since long ago; for long

yse ice

y-wis certainly, indeed, truly

Index of First Lines

(First lines of refrains are indexed in italic.)